Robert Graves was born in 1895 in Wimbledon, son of Alfred Perceval Graves, the Irish writer, and Amalia Von Ranke. He went from school to the First World War, where he became a captain in the Royal Welch Fusiliers. His principal calling was poetry, and his *Selected Poems* have been published in the Penguin Poets series. Apart from a year as Professor of English Literature at Cairo University in 1926 he earned his living by writing, mostly historical novels which include: *I Claudius*; *Claudius the God*; *Count Belisarius*; *Wife to Mr Milton*; *Sergeant Lamb of the Ninth*; *Proceed, Sergeant Lamb*; *The Golden Fleece*; *They Hanged My Saintly Billy*; and *The Isles of Unwisdom*. He wrote his autobiography, *Goodbye to All That*, in 1929, and it rapidly established itself as a modern classic. *The Times Literary Supplement* acclaimed it as 'one of the most candid self-portaits of a poet, warts and all, ever painted', as well as being of exceptional value as a war document. His two most discussed non-fiction books are *The White Goddess*, which presents a new view of the poetic impulse, and *The Nazarine Gospel Restored* (with Joshua Podro), a re-examination of primitive Christianity. He translated Apuleius, Lucan and Suetonius for the Penguin Classics, and compiled the first modern dictionary of Greek Mythology, *The Greek Myths*. His translation of *The Rubáiyát of Omar Khayyám* (with Omar Ali-Shah) is also published in Penguin. He was elected Professor of Poetry at Oxford in 1961, and made an Honorary Fellow of St John's College, Oxford, in 1971.

Robert Graves died on 7 December 1985 in Majorca, his home since 1929. On his death *The Times* wrote of him, 'He will be remembered for his achievements as a prose stylist, historical novelist and memorist, but above all as the great paradigm of the dedicated poet, "the greatest love poet in English since Donne".'

Paul O'Prey is a writer and translator, whose publications include *A Reader's Guide to Graham Greene* and two volumes of Robert Graves's selected letters: *In Broken Images* and *Between Moon and Moon*; he is also the editor of Joseph Conrad's *Heart of Darkness* and Emilia Pardo Bazán's *The House of Ulloa* for Penguin Classics.

ROBERT GRAVES

S·E·L·E·C·T·E·D P·O·E·M·S

Edited with an introduction
by Paul O'Prey

PENGUIN BOOKS

PENGUIN BOOKS

Published by the Penguin Group
27 Wrights Lane, London W8 5TZ, England
Viking Penguin Inc., 40 West 23rd Street, New York, New York 10010, USA
Penguin Books Australia Ltd, Ringwood, Victoria, Australia
Penguin Books Canada Ltd, 2801 John Street, Markham, Ontario, Canada L3R 1B4
Penguin Books (NZ) Ltd, 182–190 Wairau Road, Auckland 10, New Zealand

Penguin Books Ltd, Registered Offices: Harmondsworth, Middlesex, England

This selection first published 1986
7 9 10 8 6

All the poems in this selection appear in *Robert Graves: Collected Poems 1975* (Cassell, 1975) except for the following: 'A Boy in Church', 'To Robert Nichols', 'The Legion', *Fairies and Fusiliers* (Heinemann, 1917); 'The General Elliott', 'Epitaph on an Unfortunate Artist', *On English Poetry* (Alfred Knopf, New York, 1922); 'A Lover Since Childhood, *Whipperginny* (Heinemann, 1923); 'The Clipped Stater' *Welchman's Hose* (The Fleuron, 1925); 'A Dedication of Three Hats', 'Pygmalion and Galatea', 'The Corner Knot', 'Virgil the Sorcerer', *Poems 1914–1926* (Heinemann, 1927); 'Saint', *Poems 1926–1930* (Heinemann, 1931); 'To Whom Else?', *To Whom Else?* (The Seizin Press, Deyá, Mallorca, 1931); 'The Stranger', 'Recalling War', *Collected Poems, 1938* (Cassell, 1938); and 'Conversation Piece', *Collected Poems, 1955* (Doubleday, New York, 1955)

Filmset in Linotronic Bembo by
Rowland Phototypesetting Limited, Bury St Edmunds, Suffolk
Printed and bound in Great Britain by
Hazell Watson & Viney Limited
Member of BPCC Limited
Aylesbury, Bucks, England

CONTENTS

II

IV

V

ACKNOWLEDGEMENTS

I would like to thank Beryl Graves for her help and unfailing encouragement, also John Mole and Nicholas Drake for their very helpful reactions to an early draft of this selection.

Thanks are also due to Cassell Ltd for permission to reprint the poems which appear in their *Robert Graves Collected Poems 1975*.

PAUL O'PREY

INTRODUCTION

In the introduction to his *Collected Poems 1938* Robert Graves wrote that the poems represented 'stages in a struggle to become a poet in more than the literary sense'. Graves's view of poetry as a moral system as well as a way of life in which poets and poetry are inseparable has involved him in a lifelong dedication to a quasi-religious ideal, almost in awe of the powers and responsibilities the title of poet implies for him: powers not only of craftsmanship with words, but of magic (in this lies one of several similarities between Graves and W. B. Yeats), as he described at the beginning of *The White Goddess*:

> At the age of sixty-five I am still amused at the paradox of poetry's obstinate continuance in the present phase of civilization. Though recognized as a learned profession it is the only one for the study of which no academies are open and in which there is no yard-stick, however crude, by which technical proficiency is considered measurable. 'Poets are born, not made.' The deduction that one is expected to draw from this is that the nature of poetry is too mysterious to bear examination: is, indeed, a greater mystery even than royalty, since kings can be made as well as born and the quoted utterances of a dead king carry little weight either in the pulpit or the public bar.
>
> The paradox can be explained by the great official prestige that still somehow clings to the name of poet, as it does to the name of king, and by the feeling that poetry, since it defies scientific analysis, must be rooted in some sort of magic, and that magic is disreputable. European poetic lore is, indeed,

ultimately based on magic principles, the rudiments of which formed a close religious secret for centuries but which were at last garbled, discredited and forgotten. Now it is only by rare accidents of spiritual regression that poets make their lines magically potent in the ancient sense. Otherwise, the contemporary practice of poem-writing recalls the medieval alchemist's fantastic and foredoomed experiments in transmuting base metal into gold; except that the alchemist did at least recognize pure gold when he saw and handled it. The truth is that only gold ore can be turned into gold; only poetry into poems. This book is about the rediscovery of the lost rudiments, and about the active principles of poetic magic that govern them.

The struggle to become a poet 'in more than the literary sense' and, indeed, one could say this search for the lost rudiments and magic principles of poetry, began for Graves in 1925 (at the time he was married to the artist, Nancy Nicholson) when he first met Laura Riding. The encounter with Riding's powerful and original mind revolutionized Graves's attitude to both poetry and life. He admired her more than he admired any other of his contemporaries – an admiration which survived both the unhappiness of their later years together and their final break. In *The Long Week-End*, written in 1940, a year after this break, he said of her:

> In England she was assailed as a 'leg-puller', 'crossword puzzle setter', 'Futurist', 'tiresome intellectualist', and so on: none of her books sold more than a few dozen copies . . . She was the one poet of the time who spun, like Arachne, from her own vitals without any discoverable philosophical or literary derivations: and the only one who achieved an unshakable synthesis. Unshakable, that is, if the premiss of her unique personal authority were granted, and another more startling one – that historic Time had effectively come to an end. In her *Preliminaries* to *Epilogue I* she wrote: 'All the Chinese bandits having chopped off all the foreign ears, we have time to consider not only the subject *Atrocity*, but the subject *Bandits*, and the subject *Missionaries*, and the subject *Foreigners*, and the subject

Chinese. All the politicians who are going to be elected have been elected; and all the artificial excitement in events which no one really regards as either very important or very interesting has been exhausted. All the historical events have happened.'

This left the poets the pleasant if arduous duty of reporting 'the single event possible after everything has happened: a determination of values' . . . Laura Riding was remarkable as being in the period but not of the period, and the only woman who spoke with authority in the name of Woman (as so many men in the name of Man) without either deference to the male tradition or feministic equalitarianism: a perfect original.

Graves's new 'fundamentalist' attitude to poetry, inspired by Riding, soon led him to break with all of his many literary acquaintances in London, and in 1929 he and Riding went abroad, Graves resolving never to make England his home again. They went to Deyá, a tiny fishing village in Mallorca, and lived there in splendid isolation for six years until uprooted by the Spanish Civil War. Even before then, however, their relationship had begun to sour; Riding's uncontradictable 'personal authority' and her ambition for intellectual domination became increasingly unacceptable to Graves, but it was she herself who abruptly ended their strange partnership in 1939, at the same time as she renounced her faith in poetry.

Life with Riding had been, in the last few years at least, traumatic for Graves mentally, but as a poet it had given him enormous strength. He began a new, happier life with Beryl, his second wife, and as they started a family in the forties and early fifties Graves wrote the best of his work, both in prose and verse: *Wife to Mr Milton*, *King Jesus* and *The Golden Fleece* are the most inspired and best written of his historical novels, *The White Goddess* and *The Nazarene Gospel Restored* his most important historical/mythological studies, and *Poems 1938–45* (a volume which includes 'Through Nightmare', 'Mid-Winter Waking' and 'To Juan at the Winter Solstice') shows him at the height of his poetic powers. In 1946 Graves returned to Ca Na Lluny, the house in Deyá he had shared with Riding before the war, this time with Beryl and the children, and he has lived there ever since. In 1961 he was elected to the Chair of Poetry at Oxford, and in a series of lectures delivered on visits to the University over the following five years he gave an exciting, non-academic account of poetry from the point of view of the practising, dedicated poet, and described the immense amount of concentration and hard work behind his poems. In one of the lectures he talked of the poet's 'main problem', that of inspiration:

> The writing of true poems happens so unpredictably that the poet is beset by the temptation to write when not in the mood. He may think that this can be induced by withdrawing to a glade or quiet, book-filled study, or by violent adventure among corsairs, alguazils, barmecides, and their modern equivalents. It cannot be.
>
> No poet has yet solved the main problem: how to maintain the gift of certitude. *Always to be in love*: that is one recommendation. To treat money and fame with equal nonchalance, is another. To remain independent, is a third. To prize personal honour, is a fourth. To make the English Language one's constant study, is a fifth . . . Yet lightning strikes where and when it wills. No one ever knows. It is easy to take up a pen at random and plead: 'I'm just keeping my hand in.' But nine-tenths of what passes as English poetry is the product of either careerism, or keeping one's hand in: a choice between vulgarity and banality.

The italics are mine. The ancient traditional source of poetic inspiration is the Lunar Muse and Graves decided, in the 1950s, that to maintain his own 'gift of certitude' he must be continually in love with a woman the Muse has chosen to 'possess', as he explained in the 1960 postscript to *The White Goddess*:

A Muse-poet falls in love, absolutely, and his true love is for him the embodiment of the Muse. As a rule, the power of absolutely falling in love soon vanishes; and, as a rule, because the woman feels embarrassed by the spell she exercises over her poet lover and repudiates it; he, in disillusion, turns to Apollo who, at least, can provide him with a livelihood and intelligent entertainment, and reneges before his middle twenties. But the real, perpetually obsessed Muse-poet distinguishes between the Goddess as manifest in the supreme power, glory, wisdom and love of woman, and the individual woman whom the Goddess may make her instrument for a month, a year, seven years or even more. The Goddess abides; and perhaps he will again have knowledge of her through his experience of another woman.

Graves never turned to Apollo, and the later years of his life have been fraught with drama and anxiety as he has attempted to maintain his poetic gifts by consciously exposing himself to the vicissitudes of romantic love; between 1950 and 1974 (the date of his final volume of poems) he 'experienced' the Goddess through four different 'muse-possessed' women. He thought of these in almost wholly mythological terms – as in the following letter to the poet James Reeves in 1950, describing the entry of the first 'muse', Judith, into his life:

> The Goddess has been plaguing me lately, very cruelly, and I have managed to satisfy her by two or three poems written in red arterial blood; she appeared in person in Deyá during the last full moon, swinging a Cretan axe, but is now away again. Put into historical terms the story isn't really interesting; no liaison dangerous or alteration of the local ebbs and flows. But there are the poems; their publication in my new collection is the only impingement of poetic on historical truth . . .

Reeves, who was one of Graves's closest friends, saw this new 'philosophy' as simply a twentieth-century form of *amour courtois*, and although Graves firmly denied this there are undoubtedly certain similarities even apart from the romantic vocabulary: the idealization of the beloved, the hazy confusion between erotic love, religion and myth-ology, the encroachment of allegory and dream on reality and the importance of fidelity and chastity, for, as with Riding in the thirties, these were 'muses', *not* mistresses (in his pursuit of the Goddess Graves bears a much closer resemblance to Don Quixote than to Don Juan).

This selection begins with two very early poems marking Graves's departure from Protestant Christianity, the re-ligion of his upbringing, which he later replaced with the alternative, individual 'religion' of poetry, as he wrote in a letter to his friend Julie Matthews in 1946:

> Beryl often wishes she were religious, in her low moments: this is a dreadful epoch, and religion seems to be the only thing to keep one going in bad weather of all sorts. I never have that wish; poetry has always supplied my religious needs. This may seem a stupid statement but I am realizing, have been realizing for the last three years, that real poetry, there is very little of it like the trace of gold when they wash gravel, is an epitome of the ancestral religion of Europe which made the Minoans what they were, and which was submerged by the Aryan invaders about 2000 B.C. and finally stamped out by the Christians . . .

The extension of this 'realization' to 'experiencing the Goddess' through certain women was a difficult and not altogether successful process, love being too unpredictable for any theory and none of the 'muses' behaving as myth dictated; nevertheless, they did serve as catalysts for poetry and throughout the entire experience poetry and the God-dess, Graves's metaphor for poetic truth and inspiration, remained the real object of his love and dedication.

From *Over the Brazier* in 1916 to *At the Gate* in 1974 Graves published thirty-nine separate volumes of poetry (not in-cluding selections and anthologies). As well as these he has, since 1926, periodically compiled the various editions of the *Collected Poems*, always omitting a great deal of previously published work, a practice he explained in the introduction to the 1938 edition:

> Briefly: I have suppressed whatever I felt misrepresented my poetic seriousness at the time when it was written. This may seem self-protective; but the publication of poems should not be an act of martyrdom to the pleasure that readers may derive from one's mistakes and digressions. The temptation to digress has always vexed me . . .

Unfortunately, when the time came to edit the 1975 edition of the *Collected Poems*, Graves, by then in his eighties, felt he could no longer trust his own judgement so decided to publish *all* the later poems; this not only made the book 'top-heavy' but meant that the 'real poems', as he calls them, were obscured among the rather large quantity of 'mistakes and digressions'. To unclutter the second half of *Collected Poems 1975* has been, therefore, my main task: to make at least an initial attempt at separating the poems from the digressions since 1957, the year in which he compiled the first edition of the Penguin *Selected Poems*. He did revise and enlarge this selection in 1966, but in doing so he made only a tentative selection of the recently published poems, and the post-1957 poems have never received the severe and cold-blooded pruning from Graves that earlier work was subjected to and which he himself considers to be essential.

In making my selection I have also gone back through all the original volumes since 1916, for a reconsideration of the discarded poems, and have restored a number which seemed to me to deserve a new lease of life: very early poems such as 'A Boy in Church', 'To Robert Nichols' and 'The Legion'; and, later on, 'Epitaph on an Unfortunate Artist', 'The Corner Knot', 'The Clipped Stater', 'To Whom Else?', 'Recalling War', and seven others. On the other hand, I have also decided to omit, for various reasons, a few pre-1957 poems which appeared in Graves's Penguin *Selected Poems*.

For example, 'In Procession' (1921), an 89-line poem about Graves's severe post-war neuroses, defeated by its too-easy rhyme and indulgent nostalgia for nursery escapism; the same applies to 'The Land of Whipperginny', which has also been omitted:

> Come closer yet, my honeysuckle, my sweetheart Jinny:
> A low sun is gilding the bloom of the wood –
> Is it Heaven, or Hell, or the Land of Whipperginny
> That holds this fairy lustre, not understood.

Another example is 'Sea Side' (originally called 'Sandhills' and published in *Poems 1929*): this is an expression of Graves's distaste for the unstoppable overcrowding and loss of individualism in society, which now seems heavy-handed and indeed appears to be one of the very few occasions on which Siegfried Sassoon's jibe against Graves – that at this time he was talking 'through someone else's bonnet' – has some justification:

> The beast with two backs is a single beast,
> Yet by his love of singleness increased
> To two and two and two and two again,
> Until, instead of sandhills, see, a plain
> Patterned in two and two, by two and two –
> And the sea parts in horror at a view
> Of rows of houses coupling, back to back,
> While love smokes from their common chimney-stack
> With two-four-eight-sixteenish single same
> Re-registration of the duple name.

This is, therefore, an entirely new selection of Graves's poems, wholly independent of those made by Graves himself over the years. It is presumptuous to claim to have chosen the 'best' work of any poet, and when that poet is still alive such a claim is particularly unacceptable. Poetry is the most private art, and this can be nothing more, therefore, than a personal choice of Robert Graves's poems. Any

more authoritative – or presumptuous – claim, other than
that of personal preference, belongs to the natural selection
process of literary history.

PAUL O'PREY

I

A BOY IN CHURCH

'Gabble-gabble, . . . brethren, . . . gabble-gabble!'
  My window frames forest and heather.
I hardly hear the tuneful babble,
  Not knowing nor much caring whether
The text is praise or exhortation,
Prayer or thanksgiving, or damnation.

Outside it blows wetter and wetter,
  The tossing trees never stay still.
I shift my elbows to catch better
  The full round sweep of heathered hill.
The tortured copse bends to and fro
In silence like a shadow-show.

The parson's voice runs like a river
  Over smooth rocks. I like this church:
The pews are staid, they never shiver,
  They never bend or sway or lurch.
'Prayer,' says the kind voice, 'is a chain
That draws down grace from Heaven again.'

I add the hymns up, over and over,
  Until there's not the least mistake.
Seven-seventy-one. (Look! There's a plover!
  It's gone!) Who's that Saint by the lake?
The red light from his mantle passes
Across the broad memorial brasses.

It's pleasant here for dreams and thinking,
  Lolling and letting reason nod,
With ugly serious people linking
  Sad prayers to a forgiving God . . .
But a dumb blast sets the trees swaying
With furious zeal like madmen praying.

IN THE WILDERNESS

He, of his gentleness,
Thirsting and hungering
Walked in the wilderness;
Soft words of grace he spoke
Unto lost desert-folk
That listened wondering.
He heard the bittern call
From ruined palace-wall,
Answered him brotherly;
He held communion
With the she-pelican
Of lonely piety.
Basilisk, cockatrice,
Flocked to his homilies,
With mail of dread device,
With monstrous barbèd stings,
With eager dragon-eyes;
Great bats on leathern wings
And old, blind, broken things
Mean in their miseries.

Then ever with him went,
Of all his wanderings
Comrade, with ragged coat,
Gaunt ribs – poor innocent –
Bleeding foot, burning throat,
The guileless young scapegoat:
For forty nights and days
Followed in Jesus' ways,
Sure guard behind him kept,
Tears like a lover wept.

THE HAUNTED HOUSE

'Come, surly fellow, come: a song!'
    What, fools? Sing to you?
Choose from the clouded tales of wrong
    And terror I bring to you:

Of a night so torn with cries,
    Honest men sleeping
Start awake with rabid eyes,
    Bone-chilled, flesh creeping,

Of spirits in the web-hung room
    Up above the stable,
Groans, knockings in the gloom,
    The dancing table,

Of demons in the dry well
    That cheep and mutter,
Clanging of an unseen bell,
    Blood choking the gutter,

Of lust frightful, past belief,
    Lurking unforgotten,
Unrestrainable endless grief
    In breasts long rotten.

A song? What laughter or what song
    Can this house remember?
Do flowers and butterflies belong
    To a blind December?

TO ROBERT NICHOLS

(From Frise on the Somme in February 1917, in answer
to a letter saying: 'I am just finishing my "Faun's Holiday".
I wish you were here to feed him with cherries.')

Here by a snowbound river
In scrapen holes we shiver,
And like old bitterns we
Boom to you plaintively:
Robert, how can I rhyme
Verses for your desire –
Sleek fauns and cherry-time,
Vague music and green trees,
Hot sun and gentle breeze,

England in June attire,
And life born young again,
For your gay goatish brute
Drunk with warm melody
Singing on beds of thyme
With red and rolling eye,
Waking with wanton lute
All the Devonian plain,
Lips dark with juicy stain,
Ears hung with bobbing fruit?
Why should I keep him time?
Why in this cold and rime,
Where even to dream is pain?
No, Robert, there's no reason:
Cherries are out of season,
Ice grips at branch and root,
And singing birds are mute.

THE LEGION

'Is that the Three-and-Twentieth, Strabo mine,
Marching below, and we still gulping wine?'
From the sad magic of his fragrant cup
The red-faced old centurion started up,
Cursed, battered on the table. 'No,' he said,
'Not that! The Three-and-Twentieth Legion's dead,
Dead in the first year of this damned campaign –
The Legion's dead, dead, and won't rise again.

31

Pity? Rome pities her brave lads that die,
But we need pity also, you and I,
Whom Gallic spear and Belgian arrow miss,
Who live to see the Legion come to this,
Unsoldierlike, slovenly, bent on loot,
Grumblers, diseased, unskilled to thrust or shoot.
O brown cheek, muscled shoulder, sturdy thigh!
Where are they now? God! watch it straggle by,
The sullen pack of ragged ugly swine.
Is that the Legion, Gracchus? Quick, the wine!'
'Strabo,' said Gracchus, 'you are strange tonight.
The Legion is the Legion, it's all right.
If these new men are slovenly, in your thinking,
Hell take it! you'll not better them by drinking.
They all try, Strabo; trust their hearts and hands.
The Legion is the Legion while Rome stands,
And these same men before the autumn's fall
Shall bang old Vercingetorix out of Gaul.'

A DEDICATION OF THREE HATS

This round hat I devote to Mars,
    Though steel with leather lined.
My skin's my own, redeemed by scars
From further still more futile wars
    The God may have in mind.

Minerva takes my square of black
   Well tassled with the same;
Her dullest nurselings never lack
With hoods of scarlet at their back
   And letters to their name.

But this third hat, the foolscap sheet,
   (For there's a strength in three)
Unblemished, conical and neat
I hang up here without deceit
   To kind Euphrosyne.

Goddess, accept with smiles or tears
   This gift of a gross fool
Who having sweated in death fears
With wounds and cramps for three long years
   Limped back, and sat for school.

ONE HARD LOOK

Small gnats that fly
In hot July
And lodge in sleeping ears,
Can rouse therein
A trumpet's din
With Day of Judgement fears.

Small mice at night
Can wake more fright
Than lions at midday;
A straw will crack
The camel's back –
There is no easier way.

One smile relieves
A heart that grieves
Though deadly sad it be,
And one hard look
Can close the book
That lovers love to see.

OUTLAWS

Owls – they whinny down the night;
   Bats go zigzag by.
Ambushed in shadow beyond sight
   The outlaws lie.

Old gods, tamed to silence, there
   In the wet woods they lurk,
Greedy of human stuff to snare
   In nets of murk.

Look up, else your eye will drown
 In a moving sea of black;
Between the tree-tops, upside down,
 Goes the sky-track.

Look up, else your feet will stray
 Into that ambuscade
Where spider-like they trap their prey
 With webs of shade.

For though creeds whirl away in dust,
 Faith dies and men forget,
These agèd gods of power and lust
 Cling to life yet –

Old gods almost dead, malign,
 Starving for unpaid dues:
Incense and fire, salt, blood and wine
 And a drumming muse,

Banished to woods and a sickly moon,
 Shrunk to mere bogey things,
Who spoke with thunder once at noon
 To prostrate kings:

With thunder from an open sky
 To warrior, virgin, priest,
Bowing in fear with a dazzled eye
 Towards the dread East –

Proud gods, humbled, sunk so low,
 Living with ghosts and ghouls,
And ghosts of ghosts and last year's snow
 And dead toadstools.

ALLIE

Allie, call the birds in,
   The birds from the sky!
Allie calls, Allie sings,
   Down they all fly:
First there came
Two white doves,
   Then a sparrow from his nest,
Then a clucking bantam hen,
   Then a robin red-breast.

Allie, call the beasts in,
   The beasts, every one!
Allie calls, Allie sings,
   In they all run:
First there came
Two black lambs,
   Then a grunting Berkshire sow,
Then a dog without a tail,
   Then a red and white cow.

Allie, call the fish up,
   The fish from the stream!
Allie calls, Allie sings,
   Up they all swim:
First there came
Two gold fish,
   A minnow and a miller's thumb,
Then a school of little trout,
   Then the twisting eels come.

Allie, call the children,
    Call them from the green!
Allie calls, Allie sings,
    Soon they run in:
First there came
Tom and Madge,
    Kate and I who'll not forget
How we played by the water's edge
    Till the April sun set.

ROCKY ACRES

This is a wild land, country of my choice,
With harsh craggy mountain, moor ample and bare.
Seldom in these acres is heard any voice
But voice of cold water that runs here and there
Through rocks and lank heather growing without care.
No mice in the heath run, no song-birds fly
For fear of the buzzard that floats in the sky.

He soars and he hovers, rocking on his wings,
He scans his wide parish with a sharp eye,
He catches the trembling of small things,
He tears them in pieces, dropping them from the sky;
Tenderness and pity the heart will deny,
Where life is but nourished by water and rock –
A hardy adventure, full of fear and shock.

Time has never journeyed to this lost land,
Crakeberry and heather bloom out of date,
The rocks jut, the streams flow singing on either hand,
Careless if the season be early or late,
The skies wander overhead, now blue, now slate;
Winter would be known by his cutting snow
If June did not borrow his armour also.

Yet this is my country, beloved by me best,
The first land that rose from Chaos and the Flood,
Nursing no valleys for comfort and rest,
Trampled by no shod hooves, bought with no blood.
Sempiternal country whose barrows have stood
Stronghold for demigods when on earth they go,
Terror for fat burghers on far plains below.

REPROACH

Your grieving moonlight face looks down
   Through the forest of my fears,
Crowned with a spiny bramble-crown,
   Bedewed with evening tears.

Why do you say 'untrue, unkind',
   Reproachful eyes that vex my sleep?
Straining in memory, I can find
   No cause why you should weep.

Untrue? But when, what broken oath?
  Unkind? I know not even your name.
Unkind, untrue, you brand me both,
  Scalding my heart with shame.

The black trees shudder, dropping snow,
  The stars tumble and spin.
Speak, speak, or how may a child know
  His ancestral sin?

LOVE WITHOUT HOPE

Love without hope, as when the young bird-catcher
Swept off his tall hat to the Squire's own daughter,
So let the imprisoned larks escape and fly
Singing about her head, as she rode by.

RETURN

The seven years' curse is ended now
That drove me forth from this kind land,
From mulberry-bough and apple-bough
And gummy twigs the west wind shakes,
To drink the brine from crusted lakes
And grit my teeth on sand.

Now for your cold, malicious brain
And most uncharitable, cold heart,
You, too, shall clank the seven years' chain
On sterile ground for all time cursed
With famine's itch and flames of thirst,
The blank sky's counterpart.

The load that from my shoulder slips
Straightway upon your own is tied:
You, too, shall scorch your finger-tips
With scrabbling on the desert's face
Such thoughts I had of this green place,
Sent scapegoat for your pride.

Here, Robin on a tussock sits,
And Cuckoo with his call of hope
Cuckoos awhile, then off he flits,
While peals of dingle-dongle keep
Troop-discipline among the sheep
That graze across the slope.

A brook from fields of gentle sun
Through the glade its water heaves,
The falling cone would well-nigh stun
That Squirrel wantonly lets drop
When up he scampers to tree-top
And dives among the green.

But no, I ask a surer peace
Than vengeance on you could provide.
So fear no ill from my release:
Be off, elude the curse, disgrace
Some other green and happy place –
This world of fools is wide.

LOST LOVE

His eyes are quickened so with grief,
He can watch a grass or leaf
Every instant grow; he can
Clearly through a flint wall see,
Or watch the startled spirit flee
From the throat of a dead man.
    Across two counties he can hear
And catch your words before you speak.
The woodlouse or maggot's weak
Clamour rings in his sad ear,
And noise so slight it would surpass
Credence – drinking sound of grass,

Worm talk, clashing jaws of moth
Chumbling holes in cloth;
The groan of ants who undertake
Gigantic loads for honour's sake
(Their sinews creak, their breath comes thin);
Whir of spiders when they spin,
And minute whispering, mumbling, sighs
Of idle grubs and flies.
   This man is quickened so with grief,
He wanders god-like or like thief
Inside and out, below, above,
Without relief seeking lost love.

APPLES AND WATER

Dust in a cloud, blinding weather,
   Drums that rattle and roar!
A mother and daughter stood together
   By their cottage door.

'Mother, the heavens are bright like brass,
   The dust is shaken high,
With labouring breath the soldiers pass,
   Their lips are cracked and dry.

'Mother, I'll throw them apples down,
   I'll fetch them cups of water.'
The mother turned with an angry frown,
   Holding back her daughter.

'But, mother, see, they faint with thirst,
    They march away to war.'
'Ay, daughter, these are not the first
    And there will come yet more.

'There is no water can supply them
    In western streams that flow;
There is no fruit can satisfy them
    On orchard-trees that grow.

'Once in my youth I gave, poor fool,
    A soldier apples and water;
And may I die before you cool
    Such drouth as his, my daughter.'

THE PIER-GLASS

Lost manor where I walk continually
A ghost, though yet in woman's flesh and blood.
Up your broad stairs mounting with outspread fingers
And gliding steadfast down your corridors
I come by nightly custom to this room,
And even on sultry afternoons I come
Drawn by a thread of time-sunk memory.

Empty, unless for a huge bed of state
Shrouded with rusty curtains drooped awry
(A puppet theatre where malignant fancy
Peoples the wings with fear). At my right hand
A ravelled bell-pull hangs in readiness
To summon me from attic glooms above
Service of elder ghosts; here, at my left,
A sullen pier-glass, cracked from side to side,
Scorns to present the face (as do new mirrors)
With a lying flush, but shows it melancholy
And pale, as faces grow that look in mirrors.

Is there no life, nothing but the thin shadow
And blank foreboding, never a wainscot rat
Rasping a crust? Or at the window-pane
No fly, no bluebottle, no starveling spider?
The windows frame a prospect of cold skies
Half-merged with sea, as at the first creation –
Abstract, confusing welter. Face about,
Peer rather in the glass once more, take note
Of self, the grey lips and long hair dishevelled,
Sleep-staring eyes. Ah, mirror, for Christ's love
Give me one token that there still abides
Remote – beyond this island mystery,
So be it only this side Hope, somewhere,
In streams, on sun-warm mountain pasturage –
True life, natural breath; not this phantasma.

PYGMALION AND GALATEA

Pygmalion spoke and sang to Galatea
Who, keeping to her pedestal in doubt
Of these new qualities (blood, bones and breath)
Nor yet relaxing her accustomed poise,
Her marble rigour, though alive and burning,
Heard out his melody.

As you are woman, so be lovely:
Fine hair afloat and eyes irradiate,
Long crafty fingers, fearless carriage,
And body lissom, neither small nor tall.
So be lovely!

As you are lovely, so be merciful:
Yet must your mercy abstain from pity:
Prize your self-honour, leaving me with mine:
Love if you will: or stay stone-frozen.
So be merciful!

As you are merciful, so be constant:
I ask not you should mask your comeliness,
Yet keep our love aloof and strange,
Keep it from gluttonous eyes, from stairway gossip.
So be constant!

As you are constant, so be various:
Love comes to sloth without variety.
Within the limits of our fair-paved garden
Let fancy like a Proteus range and change.
So be various!

As you are various, so be woman:
Graceful in going as well armed in doing.
Be witty, kind, enduring, unsubjected.
Without you I keep heavy house.
So be woman!

As you are woman, so be lovely:
As you are lovely, so be various,
Merciful as constant, constant as various –
So be mine, as I yours for ever.

THE TROLL'S NOSEGAY

A simple nosegay! was that much to ask?
(Winter still nagged, with scarce a bud yet showing.)
He loved her ill, if he resigned the task.
'Somewhere,' she cried, 'there must be blossom blowing.'
It seems my lady wept and the troll swore
By Heaven he hated tears: he'd cure her spleen –
Where she had begged one flower he'd shower fourscore,
A bunch fit to amaze a China Queen.

Cold fog-drawn Lily, pale mist-magic Rose
He conjured, and in a glassy cauldron set
With elvish unsubstantial Mignonette
And such vague bloom as wandering dreams enclose.
But she?
       Awed,
             Charmed to tears,
                       Distracted,
                             Yet –
Even yet, perhaps, a trifle piqued – who knows?

DOWN

Downstairs a clock had chimed, two o'clock only.
Then outside from the hen-roost crowing came.
Why should the shift-wing call against the clock,
Three hours from dawn? Now shutters click and knock,
And he remembers a sad superstition
Unfitting for the sick-bed . . . Turn aside,
Distract, divide, ponder the simple tales
That puzzled childhood; riddles, turn them over –
Half-riddles, answerless, the more intense.
Lost bars of music tinkling with no sense
Recur, drowning uneasy superstition.

Mouth open he was lying, this sick man,
And sinking all the while; how had he come
To sink? On better nights his dream went flying,
Dipping, sailing the pasture of his sleep,
But now (since clock and cock) had sunk him down
Through mattress, bed, floor, floors beneath, stairs,
    cellars,
Through deep foundations of the manse; still sinking
Through unturned earth. How had he magicked space
With inadvertent motion or word uttered
Of too-close-packed intelligence (such there are),
That he should penetrate with sliding ease
Dense earth, compound of ages, granite ribs
And groins? Consider: there was some word uttered,
Some abracadabra – then, like a stage-ghost,
Funereally with weeping, down, drowned, lost!

Oh, to be a child once more, sprawling at ease
On smooth turf of a ruined castle court!
Once he had dropped a stone between the slabs
That masked an ancient well, mysteriously
Plunging his mind down with it. Hear it go
Rattling and rocketing into secret void!
Count slowly: one, two, three! and echoes come
Fainter and fainter, merged in the general hum
Of bees and flies; only a thin draught rises
To chill the drowsy air. There he had lain
As if unborn, until life floated back
From the deep waters.
                Oh, to renew now
That bliss of repossession, kindly sun
Forfeit for ever, and the towering sky!

Falling, falling! Day closed up behind him.
Now stunned by the violent subterrene flow
Of rivers, whirling down to hiss below
On the flame-axis of this terrible earth;
Toppling upon their waterfall, O spirit . . .

THE HILLS OF MAY

Walking with a virgin heart
    The green hills of May,
Me, the Wind, she took as lover
    By her side to play,

Let me toss her untied hair,
    Let me shake her gown,
Careless though the daisies redden,
    Though the sun frown,

Scorning in her gay habit
    Lesser love than this,
My cool spiritual embracing,
    My secret kiss.

So she walked, the proud lady,
    So she danced or ran,
So she loved with a whole heart,
    Neglecting man . . .

Fade, fail, innocent stars
   On the green of May:
She has left our bournes for ever,
   Too fine to stay.

THIEF

To the galleys, thief, and sweat your soul out
With strong tugging under the curled whips,
That there your thievishness may find full play.
Whereas, before, you stole rings, flowers and watches,
Oaths, jests and proverbs,
Yet paid for bed and board like an honest man,
This shall be entire thiefdom: you shall steal
Sleep from chain-galling, diet from sour crusts,
Comradeship from the damned, the ten-year-chained –
And, more than this, the excuse for life itself
From a craft steered toward battles not your own.

THE CASTLE

Walls, mounds, enclosing corrugations
Of darkness, moonlight on dry grass.
Walking this courtyard, sleepless, in fever;
Planning to use – but by definition
There's no way out, no way out –
Rope-ladders, baulks of timber, pulleys,
A rocket whizzing over the walls and moat –
Machines easy to improvise.
                         No escape,
No such thing; to dream of new dimensions,
Cheating checkmate by painting the king's robe
So that he slides like a queen;
Or to cry, 'Nightmare, nightmare!'
Like a corpse in the cholera-pit
Under a load of corpses;
Or to run the head against these blind walls,
Enter the dungeon, torment the eyes
With apparitions chained two and two,
And go frantic with fear –
To die and wake up sweating by moonlight
In the same courtyard, sleepless as before.

NOBODY

Nobody, ancient mischief, nobody,
Harasses always with an absent body.

Nobody coming up the road, nobody,
Like a tall man in a dark cloak, nobody.

Nobody about the house, nobody,
Like children creeping up the stairs, nobody.

Nobody anywhere in the garden, nobody,
Like a young girl quiet with needlework, nobody.

Nobody coming, nobody, not yet here,
Incessantly welcomed by the wakeful ear.

Until this nobody shall consent to die
Under his curse must everyone lie —

The curse of his envy, of his grief and fright,
Of sudden rape and murder screamed in the night.

'THE GENERAL ELLIOTT'

He fell in victory's fierce pursuit,
    Holed through and through with shot;
A sabre sweep had hacked him deep
    'Twixt neck and shoulder-knot.

The potman cannot well recall,
    The ostler never knew,
Whether that day was Malplaquet,
    The Boyne, or Waterloo.

But there he hangs, a tavern sign,
    With foolish bold regard
For cock and hen and loitering men
    And wagons down the yard.

Raised high above the hayseed world
    He smokes his china pipe;
And now surveys the orchard ways,
    The damsons clustering ripe –

Stares at the churchyard slabs beyond,
    Where country neighbours lie:
Their brief renown set lowly down,
    But his invades the sky.

He grips a tankard of brown ale
    That spills a generous foam:
Oft times he drinks, they say, and winks
    At drunk men lurching home.

No upstart hero may usurp
    That honoured swinging seat;
His seasons pass with pipe and glass
    Until the tale's complete –

And paint shall keep his buttons bright
    Though all the world's forgot
Whether he died for England's pride
    By battle or by pot.

A LOVER SINCE CHILDHOOD

Tangled in thought am I,
Stumble in speech do I?
Do I blunder and blush for the reason why?
Wander aloof do I,
Lean over gates and sigh,
Making friends with the bee and the butterfly?

If thus and thus I do,
Dazed by the thought of you,
Walking my sorrowful way in the early dew,
My heart cut through and through
In this despair for you,
Starved for a word or look will my hope renew;

Give them a thought for me
Walking so miserably,
Wanting relief in the friendship of flower or tree:
Do but remember, we
Once could in love agree.
Swallow your pride, let us be as we used to be.

SONG OF CONTRARIETY

Far away is close at hand,
Close joined is far away,
Love shall come at your command
Yet will not stay.

At summons of your dream-despair
She might not disobey,
But slid close down beside you there,
And complaisant lay.

Yet now her flesh and blood consent
In the hours of day,
Joy and passion both are spent,
Twining clean away.

Is the person empty air,
Is the spectre clay,
That love, lent substance by despair,
Wanes and leaves you lonely there
On the bridal day?

FULL MOON

As I walked out that sultry night,
   I heard the stroke of one.
The moon, attained to her full height,
   Stood beaming like the sun:
She exorcized the ghostly wheat
To mute assent in love's defeat,
   Whose tryst had now begun.

The fields lay sick beneath my tread,
    A tedious owlet cried,
A nightingale above my head
    With this or that replied –
Like man and wife who nightly keep
Inconsequent debate in sleep
    As they dream side by side.

Your phantom wore the moon's cold mask,
    My phantom wore the same;
Forgetful of the feverish task
    In hope of which they came,
Each image held the other's eyes
And watched a grey distraction rise
    To cloud the eager flame –

To cloud the eager flame of love,
    To fog the shining gate;
They held the tyrannous queen above
    Sole mover of their fate,
They glared as marble statues glare
Across the tessellated stair
    Or down the halls of state.

And now warm earth was Arctic sea,
    Each breath came dagger-keen;
Two bergs of glinting ice were we,
    The broad moon sailed between;
There swam the mermaids, tailed and finned,
And love went by upon the wind
    As though it had not been.

THE CUIRASSIERS OF THE FRONTIER

Goths, Vandals, Huns, Isaurian mountaineers,
Made Roman by our Roman sacrament,
We can know little (as we care little)
Of the Metropolis: her candled churches,
Her white-gowned pederastic senators,
The cut-throat factions of her Hippodrome,
The eunuchs of her draped saloons.

Here is the frontier, here our camp and place –
Beans for the pot, fodder for horses,
And Roman arms. Enough. He who among us
At full gallop, the bowstring to his ear,
Lets drive his heavy arrows, to sink
Stinging through Persian corslets damascened,
Then follows with the lance – he has our love.

The Christ bade Holy Peter sheathe his sword,
Being outnumbered by the Temple guard.
And this was prudence, the cause not yet lost
While Peter might persuade the crowd to rescue.
Peter renegued, breaking his sacrament.
With us the penalty is death by stoning,
Not to be made a bishop.

In Peter's Church there is no faith nor truth,
Nor justice anywhere in palace or court.
That we continue watchful on the rampart
Concerns no priest. A gaping silken dragon,
Puffed by the wind, suffices us for God.
We, not the City, are the Empire's soul:
A rotten tree lives only in its rind.

VANITY

Be assured, the Dragon is not dead
But once more from the pools of peace
Shall rear his fabulous green head.

The flowers of innocence shall cease
And like a harp the wind shall roar
And the clouds shake an angry fleece.

'Here, here is certitude,' you swore,
'Below this lightning-blasted tree.
Where once it struck, it strikes no more.

'Two lovers in one house agree.
The roof is tight, the walls unshaken.
As now, so must it always be.'

Such prophecies of joy awaken
The toad who dreams away the past
Under your hearth-stone, light-forsaken,

Who knows that certitude at last
Must melt away in vanity –
No gate is fast, no door is fast –

That thunder bursts from the blue sky,
That gardens of the mind fall waste,
That fountains of the heart run dry.

SICK LOVE

O Love, be fed with apples while you may,
And feel the sun and go in royal array,
A smiling innocent on the heavenly causeway,

Though in what listening horror for the cry
That soars in outer blackness dismally,
The dumb blind beast, the paranoiac fury:

Be warm, enjoy the season, lift your head,
Exquisite in the pulse of tainted blood,
That shivering glory not to be despised.

Take your delight in momentariness,
Walk between dark and dark – a shining space
With the grave's narrowness, though not its peace.

EPITAPH ON
AN UNFORTUNATE ARTIST

He found a formula for drawing comic rabbits:
This formula for drawing comic rabbits paid,
So in the end he could not change the tragic habits
This formula for drawing comic rabbits made.

ANGRY SAMSON

Are they blind, the lords of Gaza
  In their strong towers,
Who declare Samson pillow-smothered
  And stripped of his powers?

O stolid Philistines,
  Stare now in amaze
At my foxes running in your cornfields
  With their tails ablaze,

At swung jaw-bone, at bees swarming
  In the stark lion's hide,
At these, the gates of well-walled Gaza
  A-clank to my stride.

LOVE IN BARRENNESS

Below the ridge a raven flew
And we heard the lost curlew
Mourning out of sight below.
Mountain tops were touched with snow;
Even the long dividing plain
Showed no wealth of sheep or grain,
But fields of boulders lay like corn
And raven's croak was shepherd's horn
Where slow cloud-shadow strayed across
A pasture of thin heath and moss.

The North Wind rose: I saw him press
With lusty force against your dress,
Moulding your body's inward grace
And streaming off from your set face;
So now no longer flesh and blood
But poised in marble flight you stood.
O wingless Victory, loved of men,
Who could withstand your beauty then?

IT WAS ALL VERY TIDY

When I reached his place,
The grass was smooth,
The wind was delicate,
The wit well timed,
The limbs well formed,
The pictures straight on the wall:
It was all very tidy.

He was cancelling out
The last row of figures,
He had his beard tied up in ribbons,
There was no dust on his shoe,
Everyone nodded:
It was all very tidy.

Music was not playing,
There were no sudden noises,
The sun shone blandly,
The clock ticked:
It was all very tidy.

'Apart from and above all this,'
I reassured myself,
'There is now myself.'
It was all very tidy.

Death did not address me,
He had nearly done:
It was all very tidy.
They asked, did I not think
It was all very tidy?

I could not bring myself
To laugh, or untie
His beard's neat ribbons,
Or jog his elbow,
Or whistle, or sing,
Or make disturbance.
I consented, frozenly,
He was unexceptionable:
It was all very tidy.

ALICE

When that prime heroine of our nation, Alice,
Climbing courageously in through the Palace
Of Looking Glass, found it inhabited
By chessboard personages, white and red,
Involved in never-ending tournament,
She being of a speculative bent
Had long foreshadowed something of the kind,
Asking herself: 'Suppose I stood behind
And viewed the fireplace of Their drawing-room
From hearthrug level, why must I assume
That what I'd see would need to correspond
With what I now see? And the rooms beyond?'

Proved right, yet not content with what she had done,
Alice decided to prolong her fun:
She set herself, with truly British pride
In being a pawn and playing for her side,
And simple faith in simple stratagem,
To learn the rules and moves and perfect them.
So prosperously there she settled down
That six moves only and she'd won her crown –
A triumph surely! But her greater feat
Was rounding these adventures off complete:
Accepting them, when safe returned again,
As queer but true – not only in the main
True, but as true as anything you'd swear to,
The usual three dimensions you are heir to.
For Alice though a child could understand
That neither did this chance-discovered land
Make nohow or contrariwise the clean
Dull round of mid-Victorian routine,

Nor did Victoria's golden rule extend
Beyond the glass: it came to the dead end
Where empty hearses turn about; thereafter
Begins that lubberland of dream and laughter,
The red-and-white-flower-spangled hedge, the grass
Where Apuleius pastured his Gold Ass,
Where young Gargantua made whole holiday . . .
But farther from our heroine not to stray,
Let us observe with what uncommon sense –
Though a secure and easy reference
Between Red Queen and Kitten could be found –
She made no false assumption on that ground
(A trap in which the scientist would fall)
That queens and kittens are identical.

THE PRESENCE

Why say 'death'? Death is neither harsh nor kind:
Other pleasures or pains could hold the mind
If she were dead. For dead is gone indeed,
Lost beyond recovery and need,
Discarded, ended, rotted underground –
Of whom no personal feature could be found
To stand out from the soft blur evenly spread
On memory, if she were truly dead.

But living still, barred from accustomed use
Of body and dress and motion, with profuse
Reproaches (since this anguish of her grew
Do I still love her as I swear I do?)
She fills the house and garden terribly
With her bewilderment, accusing me,
Till every stone and flower, table and book,
Cries out her name, pierces me with her look,
'You are deaf, listen!
You are blind, see!'
                              How deaf or blind,
When horror of the grave maddens the mind
With those same pangs that lately choked her breath,
Altered her substance, and made sport of death?

THE CLIPPED STATER

(To Aircraftman 338171, T. E. Shaw)

King Alexander had been deified
By loud applause of the Macedonian phalanx,
By sullen groans of the wide worlds lately conquered.
Who but a god could have so engulphed their pride?

He did not take a goddess to his throne
In the elder style, remembering what disasters
Juno's invidious eye brought on her Consort.
Thais was fair; but he must hold his own.

Nor would he rank himself a common god
In fellowship with those of Ind or Egypt
Whom he had shamed; even to Jove his father
Paid scant respect (as Jove stole Saturn's nod).

Now meditates: 'No land of all known lands
Has offered me resistance, none denied me
Infinite power, infinite thought and knowledge;
What yet awaits the assurance of my hands?'

Alexander, in a fever of mind,
Reasons: 'Omnipotence by its very nature
Is infinite possibility and purpose,
Which must embrace *that it can be confined*.

'Then finity is true godhead's final test,
Nor does it dim the glory of free being.
I must fulfil myself by self-destruction.'
The curious phrase renews his conquering zest.

He assumes man's flesh. Djinn catch him up and fly
To a land of yellow folk beyond his knowledge,
And that he does not know them, he takes gladly
For surest proof he has put his godhead by.

In Macedonia shortly it is said:
'Alexander, our god, has died of a fever;
Demi-gods parcel out his huge dominions.'
So Alexander, as god, is duly dead.

But Alexander the man, whom yellow folk
Find roving naked, armed with a naked cutlass,
Has death, which is the stranger's fate, excused him.
Joyfully he submits to the alien yoke.

He is enrolled now in the frontier-guard
With gaol-birds and the press-gang's easy captures;
Where captains who have felt the Crown's displeasure,
But have thought suicide too direct and hard,

Teach him a new tongue and the soldier's trade,
To which the trade *he* taught has little likeness.
He glories in his foolish limitations:
At every turn his hands and feet are stayed.

'Who was your father, friend?' He answers: 'Jove.'
'His father?' 'Saturn.' 'And *his* father?' 'Chaos.'
'And *his*?' Thus Alexander loses honour:
Ten fathers is the least that a man should prove.

Stripes and bastinadoes, famine and thirst –
All these he suffers, never in resolution
Shaken, nor in his heart inquiring whether
Gods by their fiats can be self-accursed.

Thus he grows grey and eats his frugal rice,
Endures his watch on the fort's icy ramparts,
Staring across the uncouth leagues of desert,
Furbishes leather and steel; or shakes the dice.

He will not dream Olympianly, nor stir
To enlarge himself with comforts or promotion,
Nor yet evade the rack when, sour of temper,
He has tweaked a corporal's nose and called him 'cur'.

His comrades mutinously demand their pay –
'We have had none since the Emperor's Coronation.
At one gold piece a year there are fifteen owing.
One-third that sum would buy us free,' they say.

The pay-sack came at length, when hope was cold,
Though much reduced in bulk since its first issue
By the Chief Treasurer; and he, be certain,
Kept back one third of the silver and all the gold.

Every official hand had dipped in the sack;
And the frontier captains, themselves disappointed
Of long arrears, took every doit remaining;
But from politeness put a trifle back.

They informed the men: 'since no pay has come through,
We will advance from our too lavish purses
To every man of the guard, a piece of silver.
Let it be repaid when you get your overdue.'

The soldiers, grumbling but much gratified
By hopes of a drink and a drab, accept the favour;
And Alexander, advancing to the pay-desk,
Salutes and takes his pittance without pride.

The coin is bored, to string with the country's bronze
On a cord, and one side scraped to glassy smoothness;
But the head, clipped of its hair and neck, bears witness
That it had a broad, more generous mintage once.

Alexander, gazing at it then,
Greets it as an Alexandrian stater
Coined from the bullion taken at Arbela.
How came it here among these slant-eyed men?

He stands in a troubled reverie of doubt
Till a whip stings his shoulders and a voice bellows:
'Are you dissatisfied, you spawn of the ditches?'
So he salutes again and turns about,

More than uncertain what the event can mean.
Was his lost Empire, then, not all-embracing?
And how can the stater, though defaced, owe service
To a power that is as if it had never been?

'Must I renew my godhead?' But well he knows
Nothing can change the finite course resolved on;
He spends the coin on a feast of fish and almonds
And back to the ramparts briskly enough he goes.

THE CORNER KNOT

I was a child and overwhelmed: Mozart
Had snatched me up fainting and wild at heart
To a green land of wonder, where estranged
I dipped my feet in shallow brooks, I ranged
Rough mountains, and fields yellow with small vetch:
Of which, though long I tried, I could not fetch
One single flower away, nor from the ground
Pocket one pebble of the scores I found
Twinkling enchanted there. So for relief
'I'll corner-knot,' said I, 'this handkerchief,
Faithful familiar that, look, here I shake
In these cool airs for proof that I'm awake.'
I tied the knot, the aspens all around
Heaved, and the river-banks were filled with sound;
Which failing presently, the insistent loud
Clapping of hands returned me to the crowd.

I felt and, fumbling, took away with me
The knotted witness of my ecstasy,
Though flowers and streams were vanished past recall,
The aspens, the bright pebbled reach and all.

But now, grown older, I suspect Mozart
Himself had been snatched up by curious art
To my green land: estranged and wild at heart
He too had crossed the brooks, essayed to pick
That yellow vetch with which the plains are thick;
And being put to it (as I had been)
To smuggle back some witness of the scene,
Had knotted up his cambric handkerchief
With common music, rippling, flat and brief;
And home again, had sighed above the score
'Ay, a remembrancer, but nothing more.'

VIRGIL THE SORCERER

Virgil, as the old Germans have related,
    Meaning a master-poet of wide fame –
And yet their Virgil stands dissociated
    From the suave hexametrist of that name,

Maro, whose golden and lick-spittle tongue
    Served Caesar's most un-Roman tyrannies,
Whose easy-flowing Georgics are yet sung
    As declamations in the academies –

Not Mantuan Virgil but another greater
    Who at Toledo first enlarged his spells,
Virgil, sorcerer, prestidigitator,
    Armed with all power that flatters or compels.

He, says the allegory, once was thrown
    By envious dukes into a dungeon keep
Where, vermin-scarred and wasting to the bone,
    Men crouched in year-old filth and could not sleep.

He beckoned then his bond-mates to his side,
    Commanding charcoal; from a rusty grate
Charcoal they fetched him. Once again he cried
    'Where are the lordly souls, unbowed by fate,

'Eager to launch with me on midnight air
    A ship of hope, through the cold clouds to skim?'
They gazed at Virgil in a quick despair
    Thinking him mad; yet gently humoured him,

And watched his hand where on the prison wall
    He scratched a galley, buoyant and well-found.
'Bring sticks for oars!' They brought them at his call.
    'Up then and row!' They stepped from solid ground,

Climbed into fantasy and with a cheer
    Heaved anchor, bent their oars, pulled without stop.
Virgil was captain, Virgil took the steer
    And beached them, presently, on a mountain-top.

Here, without disillusion, all were free:
    Wrenching their fetters off they went their ways.
A feat, they swore, that though it could not be,
    Was, in effect, accomplished beyond praise.

Did Virgil do what legend has related?
   Is poetry in truth the queen of arts?
Can we hope better than a glib, bald-pated
   Self-laurelled Maro of agreeable parts?

Ah, fellow-captives, must you still condone
   The stench of evil? On a mound of mud
You loll red-eyed and wan, whittling a bone,
   Vermined, the low gaol-fever in your blood.

SULLEN MOODS

Love, do not count your labour lost
   Though I turn sullen or retired
Even at your side; my thought is crossed
   With fancies by no evil fired.

And when I answer you, some days,
   Vaguely and wildly, do not fear
That my love walks forbidden ways,
   Breaking the ties that hold it here.

If I speak gruffly, this mood is
   Mere indignation at my own
Shortcomings, plagues, uncertainties:
   I forget the gentler tone.

You, now that you have come to be
   My one beginning, prime and end,
I count at last as wholly me,
   Lover no longer nor yet friend.

Help me to see you as before
   When overwhelmed and dead, almost,
I stumbled on that secret door
   Which saves the live man from the ghost.

Be once again the distant light,
   Promise of glory, not yet known
In full perfection – wasted quite
   When on my imperfection thrown.

PURE DEATH

We looked, we loved, and therewith instantly
Death became terrible to you and me.
By love we disenthralled our natural terror
From every comfortable philosopher
Or tall, grey doctor of divinity:
Death stood at last in his true rank and order.

It happened soon, so wild of heart were we,
Exchange of gifts grew to a malady:
Their worth rose always higher on each side
Till there seemed nothing but ungivable pride
That yet remained ungiven, and this degree
Called a conclusion not to be denied.

Then we at last bethought ourselves, made shift
And simultaneously this final gift
Gave: each with shaking hands unlocks
The sinister, long, brass–bound coffin-box,
Unwraps pure death, with such bewilderment
As greeted our love's first acknowledgement.

WARNING TO CHILDREN

Children, if you dare to think
Of the greatness, rareness, muchness,
Fewness of this precious only
Endless world in which you say
You live, you think of things like this:
Blocks of slate enclosing dappled
Red and green, enclosing tawny
Yellow nets, enclosing white
And black acres of dominoes,
Where a neat brown paper parcel
Tempts you to untie the string.

In the parcel a small island,
On the island a large tree,
On the tree a husky fruit.
Strip the husk and pare the rind off:
In the kernel you will see
Blocks of slate enclosed by dappled
Red and green, enclosed by tawny
Yellow nets, enclosed by white
And black acres of dominoes,
Where the same brown paper parcel –
Children, leave the string alone!
For who dares undo the parcel
Finds himself at once inside it,
On the island, in the fruit,
Blocks of slate about his head,
Finds himself enclosed by dappled
Green and red, enclosed by yellow
Tawny nets, enclosed by black
And white acres of dominoes,
With the same brown paper parcel
Still unopened on his knee.
And, if he then should dare to think
Of the fewness, muchness, rareness,
Greatness of this endless only
Precious world in which he says
He lives – he then unties the string.

THE COOL WEB

Children are dumb to say how hot the day is,
How hot the scent is of the summer rose,
How dreadful the black wastes of evening sky,
How dreadful the tall soldiers drumming by.

But we have speech, to chill the angry day,
And speech, to dull the rose's cruel scent.
We spell away the overhanging night,
We spell away the soldiers and the fright.

There's a cool web of language winds us in,
Retreat from too much joy or too much fear:
We grow sea-green at last and coldly die
In brininess and volubility.

But if we let our tongues lose self-possession,
Throwing off language and its watery clasp
Before our death, instead of when death comes,
Facing the wide glare of the children's day,
Facing the rose, the dark sky and the drums,
We shall go mad no doubt and die that way.

CHILDREN OF DARKNESS

We spurred our parents to the kiss,
Though doubtfully they shrank from this –
Day had no courage to pursue
What lusty dark alone might do:
Then were we joined from their caress
In heat of midnight, one from two.

This night-seed knew no discontent:
In certitude our changings went.
Though there were veils about his face,
With forethought, even in that pent place,
Down toward the light his way we bent
To kingdoms of more ample space.

Is Day prime error, that regret
For Darkness roars unstifled yet?
That in this freedom, by faith won,
Only acts of doubt are done?
That unveiled eyes with tears are wet:
We loathe to gaze upon the sun?

THE BARDS

The bards falter in shame, their running verse
Stumbles, with marrow-bones the drunken diners
Pelt them for their delay.
It is a something fearful in the song
Plagues them – an unknown grief that like a churl
Goes commonplace in cowskin
And bursts unheralded, crowing and coughing,
An unpilled holly-club twirled in his hand,
Into their many-shielded, samite-curtained,
Jewel-bright hall where twelve kings sit at chess
Over the white-bronze pieces and the gold;
And by a gross enchantment
Flails down the rafters and leads off the queens –
The wild-swan-breasted, the rose-ruddy-cheeked
Raven-haired daughters of their admiration –
To stir his black pots and to bed on straw.

II

SAINT

This Blatant Beast was finally overcome
And in no secret tourney: wit and fashion
Flocked out and for compassion
Wept as the Red Cross Knight urged the blade home.

The people danced and sang the triumphs due,
Roasting whole oxen on the public spit;
Twelve mountain peaks were lit
With bonfires. Yet their hearts were doubt and rue.

Therefore no grave was deep enough to hold
The Beast, who after days came thrusting out,
Wormy from rump to snout,
His yellow cere-cloth patched with the grave's mould.

Nor could sea hold him: anchored with huge rocks,
He swelled and buoyed them up, paddling to shore
As evident as before
With deep-sea ooze and salty creaking bones.

Lime could not burn him, nor the sulphur-fire:
So often as the good knight bound him there,
With stink of singeing hair
And scorching flesh the corpse rolled from the pyre.

In the city-gutter would the Beast lie
Praising the Knight for all his valorous deeds:
'Ay, on those water-meads
He slew even me. These death-wounds testify.'

The Knight governed that city, a man shamed
And shrunken: for the Beast was over-dead,
With wounds no longer red
But gangrenous and loathsome and inflamed.

Not all the righteous judgements he could utter,
Nor mild laws frame, nor public works repair,
Nor wars wage, in despair,
Could bury that same Beast, crouched in the gutter.

A fresh remembrance-banquet to forestall,
The Knight turned hermit, went without farewell
To a far mountain-cell;
But the Beast followed as his seneschal,

And there drew water for him and hewed wood
With vacant howling laughter; else all day
Noisome with long decay
Sunning himself at the cave's entry stood.

He would bawl to pilgrims for a dole of bread
To feed the sick saint who once vanquished him
With spear so stark and grim;
Would set a pillow of grass beneath his head,
Would fetch him fever-wort from the pool's brim –
And crept into his grave when he was dead.

THE FURIOUS VOYAGE

So, overmasterful, to sea!
But hope no distant view of sail,
No growling ice, nor weed, nor whale,
Nor breakers perilous on the lee.

Though you enlarge your angry mind
Three leagues and more about the ship
And stamp till every puncheon skip,
The wake runs evenly behind.

And it has width enough for you,
This vessel, dead from truck to keel
With its unmanageable wheel,
A blank chart and a surly crew,

In ballast only due to fetch
The turning point of wretchedness
On an uncoasted, featureless
And barren ocean of blue stretch.

SONG: LIFT-BOY

Let me tell you the story of how I began:
I began as the boot-boy and ended as the boot-man,
With nothing in my pockets but a jack-knife and a button,
With nothing in my pockets but a jack-knife and a button,
With nothing in my pockets.

Let me tell you the story of how I went on:
I began as the lift-boy and ended as the lift-man,
With nothing in my pockets but a jack-knife and a button,
With nothing in my pockets but a jack-knife and a button,
With nothing in my pockets.

I found it very easy to whistle and play
With nothing in my head or my pockets all day,
With nothing in my pockets.

But along came Old Eagle, like Moses or David;
He stopped at the fourth floor and preached me
   Damnation:
'Not a soul shall be savèd, not one shall be savèd.
The whole First Creation shall forfeit salvation:
From knife-boy to lift-boy, from ragged to regal,
Not one shall be savèd, not you, not Old Eagle,
No soul on earth escapeth, even if all repent –'
So I cut the cords of the lift and down we went,
With nothing in our pockets.

THE READER OVER MY SHOULDER

You, reading over my shoulder, peering beneath
My writing arm – I suddenly feel your breath
   Hot on my hand or on my nape,
So interrupt my theme, scratching these few
Words on the margin for you, namely you,
   Too-human shape fixed in that shape: –

All the saying of things against myself
And for myself I have well done myself.
　　What now, old enemy, shall you do
But quote and underline, thrusting yourself
Against me, as ambassador of myself,
　　In damned confusion of myself and you?

For you in strutting, you in sycophancy,
Have played too long this other self of me,
　　Doubling the part of judge and patron
With that of creaking grind-stone to my wit.
Know me, have done: I am a proud spirit
　　And you for ever clay. Have done!

GARDENER

Loveliest flowers, though crooked in their border,
And glorious fruit, dangling from ill-pruned boughs –
Be sure the gardener had not eye enough
To wheel a barrow between the broadest gates
Without a clumsy scraping.

Yet none could think it simple awkwardness;
And when he stammered of a garden-guardian,
Said the smooth lawns came by angelic favour,
The pinks and pears in spite of his own blunders,
They nudged at this conceit.

Well, he had something, though he called it nothing –
An ass's wit, a hairy-belly shrewdness
That would appraise the intentions of an angel
By the very yard-stick of his own confusion,
And bring the most to pass.

THE LEGS

There was this road,
And it led up-hill,
And it led down-hill,
And round and in and out.

And the traffic was legs,
Legs from the knees down,
Coming and going,
Never pausing.

And the gutters gurgled
With the rain's overflow,
And the sticks on the pavement
Blindly tapped and tapped.

What drew the legs along
Was the never-stopping,
And the senseless, frightening
Fate of being legs.

Legs for the road,
The road for legs,
Resolutely nowhere
In both directions.

My legs at least
Were not in that rout:
On grass by the road-side
Entire I stood,

Watching the unstoppable
Legs go by
With never a stumble
Between step and step.

Though my smile was broad
The legs could not see,
Though my laugh was loud
The legs could not hear.

My head dizzied, then:
I wondered suddenly,
Might I too be a walker
From the knees down?

Gently I touched my shins.
The doubt unchained them:
They had run in twenty puddles
Before I regained them.

FRONT DOOR SOLILOQUY

'Yet from the antique heights or deeps of what
Or which was grandeur fallen, sprung or what
Or which, beyond doubt I am grandeur's grandson
True to the eagle nose, the pillared neck,
(Missed by the intervening generation)
Whom large hands, long face, and long feet sort out
From which and what, to wear my heels down even,
To be connected with all reigning houses,
Show sixteen quarterings or sixty-four
Or even more, with clear skin and eyes clear
To drive the nails in and not wound the wood,
With lungs and heart sound and with bowels easy:
An angry man, heaving the sacks of grain
From cart to loft and what and what and which
And even thus, and being no Rousseauist,
Nor artists-of-the-world-unite, or which,
Or what; never admitting, in effect,
Touch anything my touch does not adorn –
Now then I dung on my grandfather's doorstep,
Which is a reasonable and loving due
To hold no taint of spite or vassalage
And understood only by him and me –
But you, you bog-rat-whiskered, you psalm-griddling,
Lame, rotten-livered, which and what canaille,
You, when twin lackeys, with armorial shovels,
Unbolt the bossy gates and bend to the task,
Be off, work out your heads from between the railings,
Lest we unkennel the mastiff and the Dane –
This house is jealous of its nastiness.'

IN BROKEN IMAGES

He is quick, thinking in clear images;
I am slow, thinking in broken images.

He becomes dull, trusting to his clear images;
I become sharp, mistrusting my broken images.

Trusting his images, he assumes their relevance;
Mistrusting my images, I question their relevance.

Assuming their relevance, he assumes the fact;
Questioning their relevance, I question the fact.

When the fact fails him, he questions his senses;
When the fact fails me, I approve my senses.

He continues quick and dull in his clear images;
I continue slow and sharp in my broken images.

He in a new confusion of his understanding;
I in a new understanding of my confusion.

ULYSSES

To the much-tossed Ulysses, never done
   With woman whether gowned as wife or whore,
Penelope and Circe seemed as one:
She like a whore made his lewd fancies run,
   And wifely she a hero to him bore.

Their counter-changings terrified his way:
   They were the clashing rocks, Symplegades,
Scylla and Charybdis too were they;
Now angry storms frosting the sea with spray
   And now the lotus island's drunken ease.

They multiplied into the Sirens' throng,
   Forewarned by fear of whom he stood bound fast
Hand and foot helpless to the vessel's mast,
Yet would not stop his ears: daring their song
   He groaned and sweated till that shore was past.

One, two and many: flesh had made him blind,
   Flesh had one pleasure only in the act,
Flesh set one purpose only in the mind –
Triumph of flesh and afterwards to find
   Still those same terrors wherewith flesh was racked.

His wiles were witty and his fame far known,
Every king's daughter sought him for her own,
   Yet he was nothing to be won or lost.
   All lands to him were Ithaca: love-tossed
He loathed the fraud, yet would not bed alone.

THE STRANGER

He noted from the hill top,
Fixing a cynic eye upon
The stranger in the distance
Up the green track approaching,
She had a sure and eager tread;
He guessed mere grace of body
Which would not for unloveliness
Of cheek or mouth or other feature
Retribution pay.

He watched as she came closer,
And half-incredulously saw
How lovely her face also,
Her hair, her naked hands.
Come closer yet, deception!
But closer as she came, the more
Unarguable her loveliness;
He frowned and blushed, confessing slowly,
No, it was no cheat.

To find her foolish-hearted
Would rid his baffled thought of her;
But there was wisdom in that brow
Of who might be a Muse.
Then all abashed he dropped his head:
For in his summer haughtiness
He had cried lust at her for whom
Through many deaths he had kept vigil,
Wakeful for her voice.

ON RISING EARLY

Rising early and walking in the garden
Before the sun has properly climbed the hill –
His rays warming the roof, not yet the grass
That is white with dew still.

And not enough breeze to eddy a puff of smoke,
And out in the meadows a thick mist lying yet,
And nothing anywhere ill or noticeable –
Thanks indeed for that.

But was there ever a day with wit enough
To be always early, to draw the smoke up straight
Even at three o'clock of an afternoon,
To spare dullness or sweat?

Indeed, many such days I remember
That were dew-white and gracious to the last,
That ruled out meal-times, yet had no more hunger
Than was felt by rising a half-hour before breakfast,
Nor more fatigue – where was it that I went
So unencumbered, with my feet trampling
Like strangers on the past?

FLYING CROOKED

The butterfly, a cabbage-white,
(His honest idiocy of flight)
Will never now, it is too late,
Master the art of flying straight,
Yet has – who knows so well as I? –
A just sense of how not to fly:
He lurches here and here by guess
And God and hope and hopelessness.
Even the aerobatic swift
Has not his flying-crooked gift.

THE DEVIL'S ADVICE TO
STORY-TELLERS

Lest men suspect your tale to be untrue,
Keep probability – some say – in view.
But my advice to story-tellers is:
Weigh out no gross of probabilities,
Nor yet make diligent transcriptions of
Known instances of virtue, crime or love.
To forge a picture that will pass for true,
Do conscientiously what liars do –
Born liars, not the lesser sort that raid
The mouths of others for their stock-in-trade:
Assemble, first, all casual bits and scraps
That may shake down into a world perhaps;

People this world, by chance created so,
With random persons whom you do not know –
The teashop sort, or travellers in a train
Seen once, guessed idly at, not seen again;
Let the erratic course they steer surprise
Their own and your own and your readers' eyes;
Sigh then, or frown, but leave (as in despair)
Motive and end and moral in the air;
Nice contradiction between fact and fact
Will make the whole read human and exact.

WM. BRAZIER

At the end of Tarriers' Lane, which was the street
We children thought the pleasantest in Town
Because of the old elms growing from the pavement
And the crookedness, when the other streets were straight,
[They were always at the lamp-post round the corner,
Those pugs and papillons and in-betweens,
Nosing and snuffling for the latest news]
Lived Wm. Brazier, with a gilded sign,
'Practical Chimney Sweep'. He had black hands,
Black face, black clothes, black brushes and white teeth;
He jingled round the town in a pony-trap,
And the pony's name was Soot, and Soot was black.
But the brass fittings on the trap, the shafts,
On Soot's black harness, on the black whip-butt,
Twinkled and shone like any guardsman's buttons.
Wasn't that pretty? And when we children jeered:

'Hello, Wm. Brazier! Dirty-face Wm. Brazier!'
He would crack his whip at us and smile and bellow,
'Hello, my dears!' [If he were drunk, but otherwise:
'Scum off, you damned young milliners' bastards, you!']

Let them copy it out on a pink page of their albums,
Carefully leaving out the bracketed lines.
It's an old story – f's for s's –
But good enough for them, the suckers.

WELSH INCIDENT

'But that was nothing to what things came out
From the sea-caves of Criccieth yonder.'
'What were they? Mermaids? dragons? ghosts?'
'Nothing at all of any things like that.'
'What where they, then?'
                              'All sorts of queer things,
Things never seen or heard or written about,
Very strange, un-Welsh, utterly peculiar
Things. Oh, solid enough they seemed to touch,
Had anyone dared it. Marvellous creation,
All various shapes and sizes, and no sizes,
All new, each perfectly unlike his neighbour,
Though all came moving slowly out together.'
'Describe just one of them.'
                              'I am unable.'
'What were their colours?'
                              'Mostly nameless colours,

95

Colours you'd like to see; but one was puce
Or perhaps more like crimson, but not purplish.
Some had no colour.'
                                    'Tell me, had they legs?'
'Not a leg nor foot among them that I saw.'
'But did these things come out in any order?
What o'clock was it? What was the day of the week?
Who else was present? How was the weather?'
'I was coming to that. It was half-past three
On Easter Tuesday last. The sun was shining.
The Harlech Silver Band played *Marchog Jesu*
On thirty-seven shimmering instruments,
Collecting for Caernarvon's (Fever) Hospital Fund.
The populations of Pwllheli, Criccieth,
Portmadoc, Borth, Tremadoc, Penrhyndeudraeth,
Were all assembled. Criccieth's mayor addressed them
First in good Welsh and then in fluent English,
Twisting his fingers in his chain of office,
Welcoming the things. They came out on the sand,
Not keeping time to the band, moving seaward
Silently at a snail's pace. But at last
The most odd, indescribable thing of all,
Which hardly one man there could see for wonder,
Did something recognizably a something.'
'Well, what?'
                        'It made a noise.'
                                                'A frightening noise?'
'No, no.'
                'A musical noise? A noise of scuffling?'
'No, but a very loud, respectable noise –
Like groaning to oneself on Sunday morning
In Chapel, close before the second psalm.'
'What did the mayor do?'
                                    'I was coming to that.'

INTERRUPTION

If ever against this easy blue and silver
Hazed-over countryside of thoughtfulness,
Far behind in the mind and above,
Boots from before and below approach trampling,
Watch how their premonition will display
A forward countryside, low in the distance –
A picture-postcard square of June grass;
Will warm a summer season, trim the hedges,
Cast the river about on either flank,
Start the late cuckoo emptily calling,
Invent a rambling tale of moles and voles,
Furnish a path with stiles.
Watch how the field will broaden, the feet nearing,
Sprout with great dandelions and buttercups,
Widen and heighten. The blue and silver
Fogs at the border of this all-grass.
Interruption looms gigantified,
Lurches against, treads thundering through,
Blots the landscape, scatters all,
Roars and rumbles like a dark tunnel,
Is gone.
                    The picture-postcard grass and trees
Swim back to central: it is a large patch,
It is a modest, failing patch of green,
The postage-stamp of its departure,
Clouded with blue and silver, closing in now
To a plain countryside of less and less,
Unpeopled and unfeatured blue and silver,
Before, behind, above.

RECALLING WAR

Entrance and exit wounds are silvered clean,
The track aches only when the rain reminds.
The one-legged man forgets his leg of wood,
The one-armed man his jointed wooden arm.
The blinded man sees with his ears and hands
As much or more than once with both his eyes.
Their war was fought these twenty years ago
And now assumes the nature-look of time,
As when the morning traveller turns and views
His wild night-stumbling carved into a hill.

What, then, was war? No mere discord of flags
But an infection of the common sky
That sagged ominously upon the earth
Even when the season was the airiest May.
Down pressed the sky and we, oppressed, thrust out
Boastful tongue, clenched fist and valiant yard.
Natural infirmities were out of mode,
For Death was young again: patron alone
Of healthy dying, premature fate-spasm.

Fear made fine bed-fellows. Sick with delight
At life's discovered transitoriness,
Our youth became all-flesh and waived the mind.
Never was such antiqueness of romance,
Such tasteless honey oozing from the heart.
And old importances came swimming back –
Wine, meat, log-fires, a roof over the head,
A weapon at the thigh, surgeons at call.
Even there was a use again for God –
A word of rage in lack of meat, wine, fire,
In ache of wounds beyond all surgeoning.

War was return of earth to ugly earth,
War was foundering of sublimities,
Extinction of each happy art and faith
By which the world had still kept head in air,
Protesting logic or protesting love,
Until the unendurable moment struck –
The inward scream, the duty to run mad.

And we recall the merry ways of guns –
Nibbling the walls of factory and church
Like a child, piecrust; felling groves of trees
Like a child, dandelions with a switch!
Machine-guns rattle toy-like from a hill,
Down in a row the brave tin-soldiers fall:
A sight to be recalled in elder days
When learnedly the future we devote
To yet more boastful visions of despair.

LOST ACRES

These acres, always again lost
    By every new ordnance-survey
And searched for at exhausting cost
    Of time and thought, are still away.

They have their paper-substitute –
    Intercalation of an inch
At the so-many-thousandth foot –
    And no one parish feels the pinch.

But lost they are, despite all care,
    And perhaps likely to be bound
Together in a piece somewhere,
    A plot of undiscovered ground.

Invisible, they have the spite
    To swerve the tautest measuring-chain
And the exact theodolite
    Perched every side of them in vain.

Yet, be assured, we have no need
    To plot these acres of the mind
With prehistoric fern and reed
    And monsters such as heroes find.

Maybe they have their flowers, their birds,
    Their trees behind the phantom fence,
But of a substance without words:
    To walk there would be loss of sense.

HELL

Husks, rags and bones, waste-paper, excrement,
    Denied a soul whether for good or evil
And casually consigned to unfulfilment,
    Are pronged into his bag by the great-devil.

Or words repeated, over and over and over,
  Until their sense sickens and all but dies,
These the same fellow like a ghoulish lover
  Will lay his hands upon and hypnotize.

From husks and rags and waste and excrement
  He forms the pavement-feet and the lift-faces;
He steers the sick words into parliament
  To rule a dust-bin world with deep-sleep phrases.

When healthy words or people chance to dine
  Together in this rarely actual scene,
There is a love-taste in the bread and wine,
  Nor is it asked: 'Do you mean what you mean?'

But to their table-converse boldly comes
  The same great-devil with his brush and tray,
To conjure plump loaves from the scattered crumbs,
  And feel his false five thousands day by day.

AT FIRST SIGHT

'Love at first sight,' some say, misnaming
Discovery of twinned helplessness
Against the huge tug of procreation.

But friendship at first sight? This also
Catches fiercely at the surprised heart
So that the cheek blanches and then blushes.

DOWN, WANTON, DOWN!

Down, wanton, down! Have you no shame
That at the whisper of Love's name,
Or Beauty's, presto! up you raise
Your angry head and stand at gaze?

Poor Bombard-captain, sworn to reach
The ravelin and effect a breach –
Indifferent what you storm or why,
So be that in the breach you die!

Love may be blind, but Love at least
Knows what is man and what mere beast;
Or Beauty wayward, but requires
More delicacy from her squires.

Tell me, my witless, whose one boast
Could be your staunchness at the post,
When were you made a man of parts
To think fine and profess the arts?

Will many-gifted Beauty come
Bowing to your bald rule of thumb,
Or Love swear loyalty to your crown?
Be gone, have done! Down, wanton, down!

NATURE'S LINEAMENTS

When mountain rocks and leafy trees
And clouds and things like these,
With edges,

Caricature the human face,
Such scribblings have no grace
Nor peace –

The bulbous nose, the sunken chin,
The ragged mouth in grin
Of cretin.

Nature is always so: you find
That all she has of mind
Is wind,

Retching among the empty spaces,
Ruffling the idiot grasses,
The sheeps' fleeces.

Whose pleasures are excreting, poking,
Havocking and sucking,
Sleepy licking.

Whose griefs are melancholy,
Whose flowers are oafish,
Whose waters, silly,
Whose birds, raffish,
Whose fish, fish.

TIME

The vague sea thuds against the marble cliffs
And from their fragments age-long grinds
Pebbles like flowers.

Or the vague weather wanders in the fields,
And up spring flowers with coloured buds
Like marble pebbles.

The beauty of the flowers is Time, death-grieved;
The pebbles' beauty too is Time,
Life-wearied.

It is easy to admire a blowing flower
Or a smooth pebble flower-like freaked
By Time and vagueness.

Time is Time's lapse, the emulsive element coaxing
All obstinate locks and rusty hinges
To loving-kindness.

And am I proof against that lovesome pair,
Old age and childhood, twins in Time,
In sorrowful vagueness?

And will I not pretend the accustomed thanks:
Humouring age with filial flowers,
Childhood with pebbles?

THE PHILOSOPHER

Three blank walls, a barred window with no view,
A ceiling within reach of the raised hands,
A floor blank as the walls.

And, ruling out distractions of the body –
Growth of the hair and nails, a prison diet,
Thoughts of escape –

Ruling out memory and fantasy,
The distant tramping of a gaoler's boots,
Visiting mice and such,

What solace here for a laborious mind!
What a redoubtable and single task
One might attempt here:

Threading a logic between wall and wall,
Ceiling and floor, more accurate by far
Than the cob-spider's.

Truth captured without increment of flies:
Spinning and knotting till the cell became
A spacious other head

In which the emancipated reason might
Learn in due time to walk at greater length
And more unanswerably.

TO BRING THE DEAD TO LIFE

To bring the dead to life
Is no great magic.
Few are wholly dead:
Blow on a dead man's embers
And a live flame will start.

Let his forgotten griefs be now,
And now his withered hopes;
Subdue your pen to his handwriting
Until it prove as natural
To sign his name as yours.

Limp as he limped,
Swear by the oaths he swore;
If he wore black, affect the same;
If he had gouty fingers,
Be yours gouty too.

Assemble tokens intimate of him –
A seal, a cloak, a pen:
Around these elements then build
A home familiar to
The greedy revenant.

So grant him life, but reckon
That the grave which housed him
May not be empty now:
You in his spotted garments
Shall yourself lie wrapped.

OGRES AND PYGMIES

Those famous men of old, the Ogres –
They had long beards and stinking arm-pits,
They were wide-mouthed, long-yarded and great-bellied
Yet not of taller stature, Sirs, than you.
They lived on Ogre-Strand, which was no place
But the churl's terror of their vast extent,
Where every foot was three-and-thirty inches
And every penny bought a whole hog.
Now of their company none survive, not one,
The times being, thank God, unfavourable
To all but nightmare shadows of their fame;
Their images stand howling on the hill
(The winds enforced against those wide mouths),
Whose granite haunches country-folk salute
With May Day kisses, and whose knobbed knees.

So many feats they did to admiration:
With their enormous throats they sang louder
Than ten cathedral choirs, with their grand yards
Stormed the most rare and obstinate maidenheads,
With their strong-gutted and capacious bellies
Digested stones and glass like ostriches.
They dug great pits and heaped huge mounds,
Deflected rivers, wrestled with the bear
And hammered judgements for posterity –
For the sweet-cupid-lipped and tassel-yarded
Delicate-stomached dwellers
In Pygmy Alley, where with brooding on them
A foot is shrunk to seven inches
And twelve-pence will not buy a spare rib.

And who would judge between Ogres and Pygmies –
The thundering text, the snivelling commentary –
Reading between such covers he will marvel
How his own members bloat and shrink again.

TO EVOKE POSTERITY

To evoke posterity
Is to weep on your own grave,
Ventriloquizing for the unborn:
'Would you were present in flesh, hero!
What wreaths and junketings!'

And the punishment is fixed:
To be found fully ancestral,
To be cast in bronze for a city square,
To dribble green in times of rain
And stain the pedestal.

Spiders in the spread beard;
A life proverbial
On clergy lips a-cackle;
Eponymous institutes,
Their luckless architecture.

Two more dates of life and birth
For the hour of special study
From which all boys and girls of mettle
Twice a week play truant
And worn excuses try.

Alive, you have abhorred
The crowds on holiday
Jostling and whistling – yet would you air
Your death-mask, smoothly lidded,
Along the promenade?

THE LAUREATE

Like a lizard in the sun, though not scuttling
When men approach, this wretch, this thing of rage,
Scowls and sits rhyming in his horny age.

His time and truth he has not bridged to ours,
But shrivelled by long heliotropic idling
He croaks at us his out-of-date humours.

Once long ago here was a poet; who died.
See how remorse twitching his mouth proclaims
It was no natural death, but suicide.

Arrogant, lean, unvenerable, he
Still turns for comfort to the western flames
That glitter a cold span above the sea.

ANY HONEST HOUSEWIFE

Any honest housewife could sort them out,
Having a nose for fish, an eye for apples.
Is it any mystery who are the sound,
And who the rotten? Never, by her lights.

Any honest housewife who, by ill-fortune,
Ever engaged a slut to scrub for her
Could instantly distinguish from the workers
The lazy, the liars and the petty thieves.

Does this denote a sixth peculiar sense
Gifted to housewives for their vestal needs?
Or is it failure of the usual five
In all unthrifty writers on this head?

TO WALK ON HILLS

To walk on hills is to employ legs
As porters of the head and heart
Jointly adventuring towards
Perhaps true equanimity.

To walk on hills is to see sights
And hear sounds unfamiliar.
When in wind the pine-tree roars,
When crags with bleatings echo,
When water foams below the fall,
Heart records that journey
As memorable indeed;
Head reserves opinion,
Confused by the wind.

A view of three shires and the sea!
Seldom so much at once appears
Of the coloured world, says heart.
Head is glum, says nothing.

Legs become weary, halting
To sprawl in a rock's shelter,
While the sun drowsily blinks
On head at last brought low –
This giddied passenger of legs
That has no word to utter.

Heart does double duty,
As heart, and as head,
With portentous trifling.
A castle, on its crag perched,
Across the miles between is viewed
With awe as across years.

Now a daisy pleases,
Pleases and astounds, even,
That on a garden lawn could blow
All summer long with no esteem.

And the buzzard's cruel poise,
And the plover's misery,
And the important beetle's
Blue–green–shiny back . . .

To walk on hills is to employ legs
To march away and lose the day.
Tell us, have you known shepherds?
And are they not a witless race,
Prone to quaint visions?
Not thus from solitude
(Solitude sobers only)
But from long hilltop striding.

NEVER SUCH LOVE

Twined together and, as is customary,
For words of rapture groping, they
'Never such love,' swore, 'ever before was!'
Contrast with all loves that had failed or staled
Registered their own as love indeed.

And was this not to blab idly
The heart's fated inconstancy?
Better in love to seal the love-sure lips,
For truly love was before words were,
And no word given, no word broken.

When the name 'love' is uttered
(Love, the near-honourable malady
With which in greed and haste they
Each other do infect and curse)
Or, worse, is written down . . .

Wise after the event, by love withered,
A 'never more!' most frantically
Sorrow and shame would proclaim
Such as, they'd swear, never before were:
True lovers even in this.

THE CLOAK

Into exile with only a few shirts,
Some gold coin and the necessary papers.
But winds are contrary: the Channel packet
Time after time returns the sea-sick peer
To Sandwich, Deal or Rye. He does not land,
But keeps his cabin: so at last we find him
In humble lodgings maybe at Dieppe,
His shirts unpacked, his night-cap on a peg,
Passing the day at cards and swordsmanship
Or merry passages with chambermaids,
By night at his old work. And all is well –
The country wine wholesome although so sharp,
And French his second tongue; a faithful valet
Brushes his hat and brings him newspapers.

This nobleman is at home anywhere,
Hîs castle being, the valet says, his title.
The cares of an estate would incommode
Such tasks as now his Lordship has in hand.
His Lordship, says the valet, contemplates
A profitable absence of some years.
Has he no friend at Court to intercede?
He wants none; exile's but another name
For an old habit of non-residence
In all but the recesses of his cloak.
It was this angered a great personage.

A JEALOUS MAN

To be homeless is a pride
To the jealous man prowling
Hungry down the night lanes,

Who has no steel at his side,
No drink hot in his mouth,
But a mind dream-enlarged,

Who witnesses warfare,
Man with woman, hugely
Raging from hedge to hedge:

The raw knotted oak-club
Clenched in the raw fist,
The ivy-noose well flung,

The thronged din of battle,
Gaspings of the throat-snared,
Snores of the battered dying,

Tall corpses, braced together,
Fallen in clammy furrows,
Male and female,

Or, among haulms of nettle
Humped, in noisome heaps,
Male and female.

He glowers in the choked roadway
Between twin churchyards,
Like a turnip ghost.

(Here, the rain-worn headstone,
There, the Celtic cross
In rank white marble.)

This jealous man is smitten,
His fear-jerked forehead
Sweats a fine musk;

A score of bats bewitched
By the ruttish odour
Swoop singing at his head;

Nuns bricked up alive
Within the neighbouring wall
Wail in cat-like longing.

Crow, cocks, crow loud,
Reprieve the doomed devil –
Has he not died enough?

Now, out of careless sleep,
She wakes and greets him coldly,
The woman at home,

She, with a private wonder
At shoes bemired and bloody –
His war was not hers.

THE FOREBODING

Looking by chance in at the open window
      I saw my own self seated in his chair
With gaze abstracted, furrowed forehead,
      Unkempt hair.

I thought that I had suddenly come to die,
      That to a cold corpse this was my farewell,
Until the pen moved slowly upon paper
      And tears fell.

He had written a name, yours, in printed letters:
      One word on which bemusedly to pore –
No protest, no desire, your naked name,
      Nothing more.

Would it be tomorrow, would it be next year?
    But the vision was not false, this much I knew;
And I turned angrily from the open window
    Aghast at you.

Why never a warning, either by speech or look,
    That the love you cruelly gave me could not last?
Already it was too late: the bait swallowed,
    The hook fast.

THE HALLS OF BEDLAM

Forewarned of madness:
In three days' time at dusk
The fit masters him.

How to endure those days?
(Forewarned is foremad)
'– Normally, normally.'

He will gossip with children,
Argue with elders,
Check the cash account.

'I shall go mad that day –'
The gossip, the argument,
The neat marginal entry.

His case is not uncommon,
The doctors pronounce;
But prescribe no cure.

To be mad is not easy,
Will earn him no more
Than a niche in the news.

Then to-morrow, children,
To-morrow or the next day
He resigns from the firm.

His boyhood's ambition
Was to become an artist –
Like any City man's.

To the walls and halls of Bedlam
The artist is welcome –
Bold brush and full palette.

Through the cell's grating
He will watch his children
To and from school.

'Suffer the little children
To come unto me
With their Florentine hair!'

A very special story
For their very special friends –
They burst in the telling:

Of an evil thing, armed,
Tap-tapping on the door,
Tap-tapping on the floor,
'On the third day at dusk.'

Father in his shirt-sleeves
Flourishing a hatchet –
Run, children, run!

No one could stop him,
No one understood;
And in the evening papers . . .

(Imminent genius,
Troubles at the office,
Normally, normally,
As if already mad.)

WITH HER LIPS ONLY

This honest wife, challenged at dusk
At the garden gate, under a moon perhaps,
In scent of honeysuckle, dared to deny
Love to an urgent lover: with her lips only,
Not with her heart. It was no assignation;
Taken aback, what could she say else?
For the children's sake, the lie was venial;
'For the children's sake', she argued with her conscience.

Yet a mortal lie must follow before dawn:
Challenged as usual in her own bed,
She protests love to an urgent husband,
Not with her heart but with her lips only;
'For the children's sake', she argues with her conscience,
'For the children' – turning suddenly cold towards them.

OR TO PERISH BEFORE DAY

The pupils of the eye expand
And from near-nothings build up sight;
The pupil of the heart, the ghost,
Swelling parades the dewy land:

With cowardice and with self-esteem
Makes terror in the track that through
The fragrant spotted pasture runs;
And a bird wails across the dream.

Now, if no heavenly window shines
Nor angel-voices cheer the way,
The ghost will overbear the man
And mark his head with fever-signs.

The flowers of dusk that he has pulled
To wonder at when morning's here
Are snail-shells upon straws of grass –
So easily the eye is gulled.

The sounding words that his mouth fill
Upon to-morrow's lip shall droop;
The legs that slide with skating ease
Be stiff to the awakened will.

Or, should he perish before day,
He leaves his lofty ghost behind
Perpetuating uncontrolled
This hour of glory and dismay.

A COUNTRY MANSION

This ancient house so notable
For its gables and great staircase,
Its mulberry-trees and alleys of clipped yew,
Humbles the show of every near demesne.

At the beginning it acknowledged owners –
Father, son, grandson –
But then, surviving the last heirs of the line,
Became a place for life-tenancy only.

At the beginning, no hint of fate,
No rats and no hauntings;
In the garden, then, the fruit-trees grew
Slender and similar in long rows.

A bedroom with a low ceiling
Caused little fret at first;
But gradual generations of discomfort
Have bred an anger there to stifle sleep.

And the venerable dining-room,
Where port in Limerick glasses
Glows twice as red reflected
In the memory mirror of the waxed table –

For a time with paint and flowered paper
A mistress tamed its walls,
But pious antiquarian hands, groping,
Rediscovered the grey panels beneath.

Children love the old house tearfully,
And the parterres, how fertile!
Married couples under the testers hugging
Enjoy carnality's bliss as nowhere else.

A smell of mould from loft to cellar,
Yet sap still brisk in the oak
Of the great beams: if ever they use a saw
It will stain, as cutting a branch from a green tree.

. . . Old Parr had lived one hundred years and five
(So to King Charles he bragged)
When he did open penance, in a sheet,
For fornication with posterity.

Old Parr died; not so the mansion
Whose inhabitants, bewitched,
Pour their fresh blood through its historic veins
And, if a tile blow from the roof, tremble.

The last-born of this race of sacristans
Broke the long spell, departed;
They lay his knife and fork at every meal
And every evening warm his bed;

Yet cannot draw him back from the far roads
For trifling by the lily-pool
Or wine at the hushed table where they meet,
The guests of genealogy.

It was his childhood's pleasure-ground
And still may claim his corpse,
Yet foster-cradle or foster-grave
He will not count as home.

This rebel does not hate the house,
Nor its dusty joys impugn:
No place less reverend could provoke
So proud an absence from it.

He has that new malaise of time:
Gratitude choking with vexation
That he should opulently inherit
The goods and titles of the extinct.

ADVOCATES

Fugitive firs and larches for a moment
Caught, past midnight, by our headlight beam
On that mad journey through unlasting lands
I cannot put a name to, years ago,
(And my companions drowsy–drunk) – those trees
Resume again their sharp appearance, perfect
Of spur and tassel, claiming memory,
Claiming affection: 'Will we be included
In the catalogue? Yes, yes?' they plead.

Green things, you are already there enrolled.
And should a new resentment gnaw in me
Against my dear companions of that journey
(Strangers already then, in thought and deed)
You shall be advocates, charged to deny
That all the good I lived with them is lost.

ON PORTENTS

If strange things happen where she is,
So that men say that graves open
And the dead walk, or that futurity
Becomes a womb and the unborn are shed,
Such portents are not to be wondered at,
Being tourbillions in Time made
By the strong pulling of her bladed mind
Through that ever–reluctant element.

THE TERRACED VALLEY

In a deep thought of you and concentration
I came by hazard to a new region:
The unnecessary sun was not there,
The necessary earth lay without care –
For more than sunshine warmed the skin
Of the round world that was turned outside-in.

Calm sea beyond the terraced valley
Without horizon easily was spread,
As it were overhead,
Washing the mountain-spurs behind me:
The unnecessary sky was not there,
Therefore no heights, no deeps, no birds of the air.

Neat outside-inside, neat below-above,
Hermaphrodizing love.
Neat this-way-that-way and without mistake:
On the right hand could slide the left glove.
Neat over-under: the young snake
Through an unyielding shell his path could break.
Singing of kettles, like a singing brook,
Made out-of-doors a fireside nook.

But you, my love, where had you then your station?
Seeing that on this counter-earth together
We go not distant from each other;
I knew you near me in that strange region,
So searched for you, in hope to see you stand
On some near olive-terrace, in the heat,
The left-hand glove drawn on your right hand,

The empty snake's egg perfect at your feet –
But found you nowhere in the wide land,

And cried disconsolately, until you spoke
Immediate at my elbow, and your voice broke
This trick of time, changing the world about
To once more inside-in and outside-out.

NEW LEGENDS

Content in you,
Andromeda serene,
Mistress of air and ocean
And every fiery dragon,
Chained to no cliff,
Asking no rescue of me.

Content in you,
Mad Atalanta,
Stooping unpausing,
Ever ahead,
Acquitting me of rivalry.

Content in you
Who made King Proteus marvel,
Showing him singleness
Past all variety.

Content in you,
Niobe of no children,
Of no calamity.

Content in you,
Helen, foiler of beauty.

THE CHINK

A sunbeam on the well-waxed oak,
  In shape resembling not at all
The ragged chink by which it broke
  Into this darkened hall,
Swims round and golden over me,
  The sun's plenipotentiary.

So may my round love a chink find:
  With such address to break
Into your grief-occluded mind
  As you shall not mistake
But, rising, open to me for truth's sake.

LIKE SNOW

She, then, like snow in a dark night,
Fell secretly. And the world waked
With dazzling of the drowsy eye,
So that some muttered 'Too much light',
And drew the curtains close.
Like snow, warmer than fingers feared,
And to soil friendly;
Holding the histories of the night
In yet unmelted tracks.

THE FALLEN TOWER OF SILOAM

Should the building totter, run for an archway!
We were there already – already the collapse
Powdered the air with chalk, and shrieking
Of old men crushed under the fallen beams
Dwindled to comic yelps. How unterrible
When the event outran the alarm
And suddenly we were free –

Free to forget how grim it stood,
That tower, and what wide fissures ran
Up the west wall, how rotten the under-pinning
At the south-eastern angle. Satire
Had curled a gentle wind around it,
As if to buttress the worn masonry;
Yet we, waiting, had abstained from satire.

It behoved us, indeed, as poets
To be silent in Siloam, to foretell
No visible calamity. Though kings
Were crowned and gold coin minted still and horses
Still munched at nose-bags in the public streets,
All such sad emblems were to be condoned:
An old wives' tale, not ours.

THE CLIMATE OF THOUGHT

The climate of thought has seldom been described.
It is no terror of Caucasian frost,
Nor yet that brooding Hindu heat
For which a loin-rag and a dish of rice
Suffice until the pestilent monsoon.
But, without winter, blood would run too thin;
Or, without summer, fires would burn too long.
In thought the seasons run concurrently.

Thought has a sea to gaze, not voyage, on;
And hills, to rough the edge of the bland sky,
Not to be climbed in search of blander prospect;
Few birds, sufficient for such caterpillars
As are not fated to turn butterflies;
Few butterflies, sufficient for such flowers
As are the luxury of a full orchard;
Wind, sometimes, in the evening chimneys; rain
On the early morning roof, on sleepy sight;
Snow streaked upon the hilltop, feeding
The fond brook at the valley-head
That greens the valley and that parts the lips;
The sun, simple, like a country neighbour;
The moon, grand, not fanciful with clouds.

THE GREAT-GRANDMOTHER

That aged woman with the bass voice
And yellowing white hair: believe her.
Though to your grandfather, her son, she lied
And to your father disingenuously
Told half the tale as the whole,
Yet she was honest with herself,
Knew disclosure was not yet due,
Knows it is due now.

She will conceal nothing of consequence
From you, her great-grandchildren
(So distant the relationship,
So near her term),
Will tell you frankly, she has waited
Only for your sincere indifference
To exorcize that filial regard
Which has estranged her, seventy years,
From the folk of her house.

Confessions of old distaste
For music, sighs and roses –
Their false-innocence assaulting her,
Breaching her hard heart;
Of the pleasures of a full purse,
Of clean brass and clean linen,
Of being alone at last;
Disgust with the ailing poor
To whom she was bountiful;
How the prattle of young children
Vexed more than if they whined;
How she preferred cats.

She will say, yes, she acted well,
Took such pride in the art
That none of them suspected, even,
Her wrathful irony
In doing what they asked
Better than they could ask it . . .
But, ah, how grudgingly her will returned
After the severance of each navel-cord,
And fled how far again,
When again she was kind!

She has outlasted all man-uses,
As was her first resolve:
Happy and idle like a port
After the sea's recession,
She does not misconceive the nature
Of shipmen or of ships.
Hear her, therefore, as the latest voice;
The intervening generations (drifting
On tides of fancy still), ignore.

NO MORE GHOSTS

The patriarchal bed with four posts
Which was a harbourage of ghosts
Is hauled out from the attic glooms
And cut to wholesome furniture for wholesome rooms;

Where they (the ghosts) confused, abused, thinned,
Forgetful how they sighed and sinned,
Cannot disturb our ordered ease
Except as summer dust tickles the nose to sneeze.

We are restored to simple days, are free
From cramps of dark necessity,
And one another recognize
By an immediate love that signals at our eyes.

No new ghosts can appear. Their poor cause
Was that time freezes, and time thaws;
But here only such loves can last
As do not ride upon the weathers of the past.

THE AGES OF OATH

To find a garden-tulip growing
Among wild primroses of a wild field,
Or a cuckoo's egg in a blackbird's nest,
Or a giant mushroom, a whole basketful –
The memorable feats of childhood!
Once, by the earthworks, scratching in the soil,
My stick turned up a Roman amber bead . . .

The lost, the freakish, the unspelt
Drew me: for simple sights I had no eye.
And did I swear allegiance then
To wildness, not (as I thought) to truth –
Become a virtuoso, and this also,
Later, of simple sights, when tiring
Of unicorn and upas?

Did I forget how to greet plainly
The especial sight, how to know deeply
The pleasure shared by upright hearts?
And is this to begin afresh, with oaths
On the true book, in the true name,
Now stammering out my praise of you,
Like a boy owning his first love?

END OF PLAY

We have reached the end of pastime, for always,
Ourselves and everyone, though few confess it
Or see the sky other than, as of old,
A foolish smiling Mary-mantle blue;

Though life may still seem to dawdle golden
In some June landscape among giant flowers,
The grass to shine as cruelly green as ever,
Faith to descend in a chariot from the sky –

May seem only: a mirror and an echo
Mediate henceforth with vision and sound.
The cry of faith, no longer mettlesome,
Sounds as a blind man's pitiful plea of 'blind'.

We have at last ceased idling, which to regret
Were as shallow as to ask our milk-teeth back;
As many forthwith do, and on their knees
Call lugubriously upon chaste Christ.

We tell no lies now, at last cannot be
The rogues we were – so evilly linked in sense
With what we scrutinized that lion or tiger
Could leap from every copse, strike and devour us.

No more shall love in hypocritic pomp
Conduct its innocents through a dance of shame,
From timid touching of gloved fingers
To frantic laceration of naked breasts.

Yet love survives, the word carved on a sill
Under antique dread of the headsman's axe;
It is the echoing mind, as in the mirror
We stare on our dazed trunks at the block kneeling.

TO WHOM ELSE?

To whom else other than,
To whom else not of man
Yet in human state,
Standing neither in stead
Of self nor idle godhead,
Should I, man in man bounded,
Myself dedicate?

To whom else momently,
To whom else endlessly,
But to you, I?
To you who only,
To you who mercilessly,
To you who lovingly,
Plucked out the lie?

To whom else less acquaint,
To whom else without taint
Of death, death-true?
With great astonishment
Thankfully I consent
To my estrangement
From me in you.

LEAVING THE REST UNSAID

Finis, apparent on an earlier page,
With fallen obelisk for colophon,
Must this be here repeated?

Death has been ruefully announced
And to die once is death enough,
Be sure, for any life-time.

Must the book end, as you would end it,
With testamentary appendices
And graveyard indices?

But no, I will not lay me down
To let your tearful music mar
The decent mystery of my progress.

So now, my solemn ones, leaving the rest unsaid,
Rising in air as on a gander's wing
At a careless comma,

III

A LOVE STORY

The full moon easterly rising, furious,
Against a winter sky ragged with red;
The hedges high in snow, and owls raving –
Solemnities not easy to withstand:
A shiver wakes the spine.

In boyhood, having encountered the scene,
I suffered horror: I fetched the moon home,
With owls and snow, to nurse in my head
Throughout the trials of a new Spring,
Famine unassuaged.

But fell in love, and made a lodgement
Of love on those chill ramparts.
Her image was my ensign: snows melted,
Hedges sprouted, the moon tenderly shone,
The owls trilled with tongues of nightingale.

These were all lies, though they matched the time,
And brought me less than luck: her image
Warped in the weather, turned beldamish.
Then back came winter on me at a bound,
The pallid sky heaved with a moon-quake.

Dangerous it had been with love-notes
To serenade Queen Famine.
In tears I recomposed the former scene,
Let the snow lie, watched the moon rise, suffered the owls,
Paid homage to them of unevent.

DAWN BOMBARDMENT

Guns from the sea open against us:
The smoke rocks bodily in the casemate
And a yell of doom goes up.
We count and bless each new, heavy concussion –
Captives awaiting rescue.

Visiting angel of the wild-fire hair
Who in dream reassured us nightly
Where we lay fettered,
Laugh at us, as we wake – our faces
So tense with hope the tears run down.

THE SHOT

The curious heart plays with its fears:
To hurl a shot through the ship's planks,
Being assured that the green angry flood
Is charmed and dares not dance into the hold –
Nor first to sweep a lingering glance around
For land or shoal or cask adrift.
'So miracles are done; but madmen drown.'

O weary luxury of hypothesis –
For human nature, honest human nature
(Which the fear-pampered heart denies)
Knows its own miracle: not to go mad.
Will pitch the shot in fancy, hint the fact,
Will bore perhaps a meagre auger hole
But stanch the spurting with a tarred rag,
And will not drown, nor even ride the cask.

TO SLEEP

The mind's eye sees as the heart mirrors:
Loving in part, I did not see you whole,
Grew flesh-enraged that I could not conjure
A whole you to attend my fever-fit
In the doubtful hour between a night and day
And be Sleep that had kept so long away.

Of you sometimes a hand, a brooch, a shoe
Wavered beside me, unarticulated –
As the vexed insomniac dream-forges;
And the words I chose for your voice to speak
Echoed my own voice with its dry creak.

Now that I love you, now that I recall
All scattered elements of will that swooped
By night as jealous dreams through windows
To circle above the beds like bats,
Or as dawn-birds flew blindly at the panes
In curiosity rattling out their brains –

Now that I love you, as not before,
Now you can be and say, as not before:
The mind clears and the heart true-mirrors you
Where at my side an early watch you keep
And all self-bruising heads loll into sleep.

THE THIEVES

Lovers in the act dispense
With such meum-tuum sense
As might warningly reveal
What they must not pick or steal,
And their nostrum is to say:
'I and you are both away.'

After, when they disentwine
You from me and yours from mine,
Neither can be certain who
Was that I whose mine was you.
To the act again they go
More completely not to know.

Theft is theft and raid is raid
Though reciprocally made.
Lovers, the conclusion is
Doubled sighs and jealousies
In a single heart that grieves
For lost honour among thieves.

LOLLOCKS

By sloth on sorrow fathered,
These dusty-featured Lollocks
Have their nativity in all disordered
Backs of cupboard drawers.

They play hide and seek
Among collars and novels
And empty medicine bottles,
And letters from abroad
That never will be answered.

Every sultry night
They plague little children,
Gurgling from the cistern,
Humming from the air,
Skewing up the bed-clothes,
Twitching the blind.

When the imbecile agèd
Are over-long in dying
And the nurse drowses,
Lollocks come skipping
Up the tattered stairs
And are nasty together
In the bed's shadow.

The signs of their presence
Are boils on the neck,
Dreams of vexation suddenly recalled
In the middle of the morning,
Languor after food.

Men cannot see them,
Men cannot hear them,
Do not believe in them –
But suffer the more
Both in neck and belly.

Women can see them –
O those naughty wives
Who sit by the fireside
Munching bread and honey,
Watching them in mischief
From corners of their eyes,
Slily allowing them to lick
Honey-sticky fingers.

Sovereign against Lollocks
Are hard broom and soft broom,
To well comb the hair,
To well brush the shoe,
And to pay every debt
As it falls due.

DESPITE AND STILL

Have you not read
The words in my head,
And I made part
Of your own heart?
We have been such as draw
The losing straw –
You of your gentleness,
I of my rashness,
Both of despair –
Yet still might share
This happy will:
To love despite and still.
Never let us deny
The thing's necessity,
But, O, refuse
To choose
Where chance may seem to give
Loves in alternative.

THE SUICIDE IN THE COPSE

The suicide, far from content,
Stared down at his own shattered skull:
Was this what he meant?

Had not his purpose been
To liberate himself from duns and dolts
By a change of scene?

From somewhere came a roll of laughter:
He had looked so on his wedding-day,
And the day after.

There was nowhere at all to go,
And no diversion now but to peruse
What literature the winds might blow

Into the copse where his body lay:
A year-old sheet of sporting news,
A crumpled schoolboy essay.

FRIGHTENED MEN

We were not ever of their feline race,
Never had hidden claws so sharp as theirs
In any half-remembered incarnation;
Have only the least knowledge of their minds
Through a grace on their part in thinking aloud;
And we remain mouse-quiet when they begin
Suddenly in their unpredictable way
To weave an allegory of their lives,
Making each point by walking round it –
Then off again, as interest is warmed.
What have they said? Or unsaid? What?
We understood the general drift only.

They are punctilious as implacable,
Most neighbourly to those who love them least.
A shout will scare them. When they spring, they seize.
The worst is when they hide from us and change
To something altogether other:
We meet them at the door, as who returns
After a one-hour-seeming century
To a house not his own.

THE OATH

The doubt and the passion
Falling away from them,
  In that instant both
Take timely courage
From the sky's clearness
  To confirm an oath.

Her loves are his loves,
His trust is her trust;
  Else all were grief
And they, lost ciphers
On a yellowing page,
  Death overleaf.

Rumour of old battle
Growls across the air;
   Then let it growl
With no more terror
Than the creaking stair
   Or the calling owl.

She knows, as he knows,
Of a faithful-always
   And an always-dear
By early emblems
Prognosticated,
   Fulfilled here.

LANGUAGE OF THE SEASONS

Living among orchards, we are ruled
By the four seasons necessarily:
This from unseasonable frosts we learn
Or from usurping suns and haggard flowers –
Legitimist our disapproval.

Weather we knew, not seasons, in the city
Where, seasonless, orange and orchid shone,
Knew it by heavy overcoat or light,
Framed love in later terminologies
Than here, where we report how weight of snow,
Or weight of fruit, tears branches from the tree.

THE BEACH

Louder than gulls the little children scream
Whom fathers haul into the jovial foam;
But others fearlessly rush in, breast high,
Laughing the salty water from their mouths –
Heroes of the nursery.

The horny boatman, who has seen whales
And flying fishes, who has sailed as far
As Demerara and the Ivory Coast,
Will warn them, when they crowd to hear his tales,
That every ocean smells alike of tar.

MID-WINTER WAKING

Stirring suddenly from long hibernation,
I knew myself once more a poet
Guarded by timeless principalities
Against the worm of death, this hillside haunting;
And presently dared open both my eyes.

O gracious, lofty, shone against from under,
Back-of-the-mind-far clouds like towers;
And you, sudden warm airs that blow
Before the expected season of new blossom,
While sheep still gnaw at roots and lambless go –

Be witness that on waking, this mid-winter,
I found her hand in mind laid closely
Who shall watch out the Spring with me.
We stared in silence all around us
But found no winter anywhere to see.

UNDER THE POT

Sulkily the sticks burn, and though they crackle
    With scorn under the bubbling pot, or spout
Magnanimous jets of flame against the smoke,
    At each heel end a dirty sap breaks out.

Confess, creatures, how sulkily ourselves
    We hiss with doom, fuel of a sodden age –
Not rapt up roaring to the chimney stack
    On incandescent clouds of spirit or rage.

THE VILLAGERS AND DEATH

The Rector's pallid neighbour at The Firs,
Death, did not flurry the parishioners.
Yet from a weight of superstitious fears
Each tried to lengthen his own term of years.
He was congratulated who combined
Toughness of flesh and weakness of the mind
In consequential rosiness of face.
This dull and not ill-mannered populace
Pulled off their caps to Death, as they slouched by,
But rumoured him both atheist and spy.
All vowed to outlast him (though none ever did)
And hear the earth drum on his coffin-lid.
Their groans and whispers down the village street
Soon soured his nature, which was never sweet.

THE DEATH ROOM

Look forward, truant, to your second childhood.
The crystal sphere discloses
Wall-paper roses mazily repeated
In pink and bronze, their bunches harbouring
Elusive faces, under an inconclusive
Circling, spidery, ceiling craquelure,
And, by the window-frame, the well-loathed, lame,
Damp-patch, cross-patch, sleepless L-for-Lemur
Who, puffed to giant size,
Waits jealously till children close their eyes.

THE DOOR

When she came suddenly in
It seemed the door could never close again,
Nor even did she close it – she, she –
The room lay open to a visiting sea
Which no door could restrain.

Yet when at last she smiled, tilting her head
To take her leave of me,
Where she had smiled, instead
There was a dark door closing endlessly,
The waves receded.

THROUGH NIGHTMARE

Never be disenchanted of
That place you sometimes dream yourself into,
Lying at large remove beyond all dream,
Or those you find there, though but seldom
In their company seated –

The untameable, the live, the gentle.
Have you not known them? Whom? They carry
Time looped so river-wise about their house
There's no way in by history's road
To name or number them.

In your sleepy eyes I read the journey
Of which disjointedly you tell; which stirs
My loving admiration, that you should travel
Through nightmare to a lost and moated land,
Who are timorous by nature.

TO LUCIA AT BIRTH

Though the moon beaming matronly and bland
   Greets you, among the crowd of the new-born,
With 'welcome to the world' yet understand
   That still her pale, lascivious unicorn
And bloody lion are loose on either hand:
   With din of bones and tantará of horn
Their fanciful cortège parades the land –
   Pest on the high road, wild-fire in the corn.

Outrageous company to be born into,
   Lunatics of a royal age long dead.
Then reckon time by what you are or do,
   Not by the epochs of the war they spread.
   Hark how they roar; but never turn your head.
Nothing will change them, let them not change you.

SHE TELLS HER LOVE WHILE HALF ASLEEP

She tells her love while half asleep,
  In the dark hours,
     With half-words whispered low:
As Earth stirs in her winter sleep
  And puts out grass and flowers
     Despite the snow,
     Despite the falling snow.

THESEUS AND ARIADNE

High on his figured couch beyond the waves
He dreams, in dream recalling her set walk
Down paths of oyster-shell bordered with flowers,
Across the shadowy turf below the vines.
He sighs: 'Deep sunk in my erroneous past
She haunts the ruins and the ravaged lawns.'

Yet still unharmed it stands, the regal house
Crooked with age and overtopped by pines
Where first he wearied of her constancy.
And with a surer foot she goes than when
Dread of his hate was thunder in the air,
When the pines agonized with flaws of wind
And flowers glared up at her with frantic eyes.

Of him, now all is done, she never dreams
But calls a living blessing down upon
What he supposes rubble and rank grass;
Playing the queen to nobler company.

INSTRUCTIONS TO THE ORPHIC ADEPT

[In part translated from the *Timpone Grande* and
Compagno Orphic tablets.]

So soon as ever your mazed spirit descends
From daylight into darkness, Man, remember
What you have suffered here in Samothrace,
What you have suffered.

After your passage through Hell's seven floods,
Whose fumes of sulphur will have parched your throat,
The Halls of Judgement shall loom up before you,
A miracle of jasper and of onyx.
To the left hand there bubbles a black spring
Overshadowed with a great white cypress.
Avoid this spring, which is Forgetfulness;
Though all the common rout rush down to drink,
Avoid this spring!

155

To the right hand there lies a secret pool
Alive with speckled trout and fish of gold;
A hazel overshadows it. Ophion,
Primaeval serpent straggling in the branches,
Darts out his tongue. This holy pool is fed
By dripping water; guardians stand before it.
Run to this pool, the pool of Memory,
Run to this pool!

Then will the guardians scrutinize you, saying:
'Who are you, who? What have you to remember?
Do you not fear Ophion's flickering tongue?
Go rather to the spring beneath the cypress,
Flee from this pool!'

Then you shall answer: 'I am parched with thirst.
Give me to drink. I am a child of Earth,
But of Sky also, come from Samothrace.
Witness the glint of amber on my brow.
Out of the Pure I come, as you may see.
I also am of your thrice-blessèd kin,
Child of the three-fold Queen of Samothrace;
Have made full quittance for my deeds of blood,
Have been by her invested in sea-purple,
And like a kid have fallen into milk.
Give me to drink, now I am parched with thirst,
Give me to drink!'

But they will ask you yet: 'What of your feet?'
You shall reply: 'My feet have borne me here
Out of the weary wheel, the circling years,
To that still, spokeless wheel: – Persephone.
Give me to drink!'

Then they will welcome you with fruit and flowers,
And lead you toward the ancient dripping hazel,
Crying: 'Brother of our immortal blood,
Drink and remember glorious Samothrace!'
Then you shall drink.

You shall drink deep of that refreshing draught,
To become lords of the uninitiated
Twittering ghosts, Hell's countless populace –
To become heroes, knights upon swift horses,
Pronouncing oracles from tall white tombs
By the nymphs tended. They with honey water
Shall pour libations to your serpent shapes,
That you may drink.

LAMENT FOR PASIPHAË

Dying sun, shine warm a little longer!
My eye, dazzled with tears, shall dazzle yours,
Conjuring you to shine and not to move.
You, sun, and I all afternoon have laboured
Beneath a dewless and oppressive cloud –
A fleece now gilded with our common grief
That this must be a night without a moon.
Dying sun, shine warm a little longer!

Faithless she was not: she was very woman,
Smiling with dire impartiality,
Sovereign, with heart unmatched, adored of men,
Until Spring's cuckoo with bedraggled plumes
Tempted her pity and her truth betrayed.
Then she who shone for all resigned her being,
And this must be a night without a moon.
Dying sun, shine warm a little longer!

TO JUAN AT THE WINTER SOLSTICE

There is one story and one story only
That will prove worth your telling,
Whether as learned bard or gifted child;
To it all lines or lesser gauds belong
That startle with their shining
Such common stories as they stray into.

Is it of trees you tell, their months and virtues,
Or strange beasts that beset you,
Of birds that croak at you the Triple will?
Or of the Zodiac and how slow it turns
Below the Boreal Crown,
Prison of all true kings that ever reigned?

Water to water, ark again to ark,
From woman back to woman:
So each new victim treads unfalteringly
The never altered circuit of his fate,
Bringing twelve peers as witness
Both to his starry rise and starry fall.

Or is it of the Virgin's silvery beauty,
All fish below the thighs?
She in her left hand bears a leafy quince;
When with her right she crooks a finger, smiling,
How may the King hold back?
Royally then he barters life for love.

Or of the undying snake from chaos hatched,
Whose coils contain the ocean,
Into whose chops with naked sword he springs,
Then in black water, tangled by the reeds,
Battles three days and nights,
To be spewed up beside her scalloped shore?

Much snow is falling, winds roar hollowly,
The owl hoots from the elder,
Fear in your heart cries to the loving-cup:
Sorrow to sorrow as the sparks fly upward.
The log groans and confesses:
There is one story and one story only.

Dwell on her graciousness, dwell on her smiling,
Do not forget what flowers
The great boar trampled down in ivy time.
Her brow was creamy as the crested wave,
Her sea-grey eyes were wild
But nothing promised that is not performed.

TO BE CALLED A BEAR

Bears gash the forest trees
    To mark the bounds
    Of their own hunting grounds;
They follow the wild bees
    Point by point home
    For love of honeycomb;
They browse on blueberries.

Then should I stare
If I am called a bear,
And it is not the truth?
Unkempt and surly with a sweet tooth
I tilt my muzzle toward the starry hub
Where Queen Callisto guards her cub;

But envy those that here
    All winter breathing slow
    Sleep warm under the snow,
That yawn awake when the skies clear,
    And lank with longing grow
No more than one brief month a year.

CONVERSATION PIECE

By moonlight
At midnight,
Under the vines,
A hotel chair
Settles down moodily before the headlines
Of a still-folded evening newspaper.

The other chair
Of the pair
Lies on its back,
Stiff as in pain,
Having been overturned with an angry crack;
And there till morning, alas, it must remain.

On the terrace
No blood-trace,
No sorry glitter
Of a knife, nothing:
Not even the fine-torn fragments of a letter
Or the dull gleam of a flung-off wedding-ring.

Still stable
On the table
Two long-stemmed glasses,
One full of drink,
Watch how the rat among the vines passes
And how the moon trembles on the crag's brink.

MY NAME AND I

The impartial Law enrolled a name
    For my especial use:
My rights in it would rest the same
Whether I puffed it into fame
    Or sank it in abuse.

Robert was what my parents guessed
    When first they peered at me,
And *Graves* an honourable bequest
With Georgian silver and the rest
    From my male ancestry.

They taught me: 'You are *Robert Graves*
    (Which you must learn to spell),
But see that *Robert Graves* behaves,
Whether with honest men or knaves,
    Exemplarily well.'

Then though my I was always I,
    Illegal and unknown,
With nothing to arrest it by –
As will be obvious when I die
    And *Robert Graves* lives on –

I cannot well repudiate
    This noun, this natal star,
This gentlemanly self, this mate
So kindly forced on me by fate,
    Time and the registrar;

And therefore hurry him ahead
    As an ambassador
To fetch me home my beer and bread
Or commandeer the best green bed,
    As he has done before.

Yet, understand, I am not he
    Either in mind or limb;
My name will take less thought for me,
In worlds of men I cannot see,
    Than ever I for him.

1805

At Viscount Nelson's lavish funeral,
    While the mob milled and yelled about St Paul's,
A General chatted with an Admiral:

'One of your Colleagues, Sir, remarked today
    That Nelson's *exit*, though to be lamented,
Falls not inopportunely, in its way.'

'He was a thorn in our flesh,' came the reply –
    'The most bird-witted, unaccountable,
Odd little runt that ever I did spy.

'One arm, one peeper, vain as Pretty Poll,
    A meddler, too, in foreign politics
And gave his heart in pawn to a plain moll.

'He would dare lecture us Sea Lords, and then
    Would treat his ratings as though men of honour
And play at leap-frog with his midshipmen!

'We tried to box him down, but up he popped,
    And when he'd banged Napoleon at the Nile
Became too much the hero to be dropped.

'You've heard that Copenhagen "blind" eye story?
    We'd tied him to Nurse Parker's apron-strings –
By G—d, he snipped them through and snatched the
      glory!'

'Yet,' cried the General, 'six-and-twenty sail
    Captured or sunk by him off Tráfalgár –
That writes a handsome *finis* to the tale.'

'Handsome enough. The seas are England's now.
    That fellow's foibles need no longer plague us.
He died most creditably, I'll allow.'

'And, Sir, the secret of his victories?'
    'By his unServicelike, familiar ways, Sir,
He made the whole Fleet love him, damn his eyes!'

THE PERSIAN VERSION

Truth-loving Persians do not dwell upon
The trivial skirmish fought near Marathon.
As for the Greek theatrical tradition
Which represents that summer's expedition
Not as a mere reconnaissance in force
By three brigades of foot and one of horse
(Their left flank covered by some obsolete
Light craft detached from the main Persian fleet)
But as a grandiose, ill-starred attempt
To conquer Greece – they treat it with contempt;
And only incidentally refute
Major Greek claims, by stressing what repute
The Persian monarch and the Persian nation
Won by this salutary demonstration:
Despite a strong defence and adverse weather
All arms combined magnificently together.

THE WHITE GODDESS

All saints revile her, and all sober men
Ruled by the God Apollo's golden mean –
In scorn of which we sailed to find her
In distant regions likeliest to hold her
Whom we desired above all things to know,
Sister of the mirage and echo.

It was a virtue not to stay,
To go our headstrong and heroic way
Seeking her out at the volcano's head,
Among pack ice, or where the track had faded
Beyond the cavern of the seven sleepers:
Whose broad high brow was white as any leper's,
Whose eyes were blue, with rowan-berry lips,
With hair curled honey-coloured to white hips.

Green sap of Spring in the young wood a-stir
Will celebrate the Mountain Mother,
And every song-bird shout awhile for her;
But we are gifted, even in November
Rawest of seasons, with so huge a sense
Of her nakedly worn magnificence
We forget cruelty and past betrayal,
Heedless of where the next bright bolt may fall.

COUNTING THE BEATS

You, love, and I,
(He whispers) you and I,
And if no more than only you and I
What care you or I?

Counting the beats,
Counting the slow heart beats,
The bleeding to death of time in slow heart beats,
Wakeful they lie.

Cloudless day,
Night, and a cloudless day,
Yet the huge storm will burst upon their heads one day
From a bitter sky.

Where shall we be,
(She whispers) where shall we be,
When death strikes home, O where then shall we be
Who were you and I?

Not there but here,
(He whispers) only here,
As we are, here, together, now and here,
Always you and I.

Counting the beats,
Counting the slow heart beats,
The bleeding to death of time in slow heart beats,
Wakeful they lie.

THE SURVIVOR

To die with a forlorn hope, but soon to be raised
By hags, the spoilers of the field, to elude their claws
And stand once more on a well-swept parade-ground,
Scarred and bemedalled, sword upright in fist
At head of a new undaunted company:

Is this joy? to be doubtless alive again,
And the others dead? Will your nostrils gladly savour
The fragrance, always new, of a first hedge-rose?
Will your ears be charmed by the thrush's melody
Sung as though he had himself devised it?

And is this joy: after the double suicide
(Heart against heart) to be restored entire,
To smooth your hair and wash away the life-blood,
And presently seek a young and innocent bride,
Whispering in the dark: 'for ever and ever'?

QUESTIONS IN A WOOD

The parson to his pallid spouse,
   The hangman to his whore,
Do both not mumble the same vows,
   Both knock at the same door?

And when the fury of their knocks
   Has waned, and that was that,
What answer comes, unless the pox
   Or one more parson's brat?

Tell me, my love, my flower of flowers,
   True woman to this man,
What have their deeds to do with ours
   Or any we might plan?

Your startled gaze, your restless hand,
   Your hair like Thames in flood,
And choked voice, battling to command
   The insurgence of your blood:

How can they spell the dark word said
   Ten thousand times a night
By women as corrupt and dead
   As you are proud and bright?

And how can I, in the same breath,
   Though warned against the cheat,
Vilely deliver love to death
   Wrapped in a rumpled sheet?

Yet, if from delicacy of pride
   We choose to hold apart,
Will no blue hag appear, to ride
   Hell's wager in each heart?

DARIEN

It is a poet's privilege and fate
To fall enamoured of the one Muse
Who variously haunts this island earth.

She was your mother, Darien,
And presaged by the darting halcyon bird
Would run green-sleeved along her ridges,
Treading the asphodels and heather-trees
With white feet bare.

Often at moonrise I had watched her go,
And a cold shudder shook me
To see the curved blaze of her Cretan axe.
Averted her set face, her business
Not yet with me, long-striding,
She would ascend the peak and pass from sight.
But once at full moon, by the sea's verge,
I came upon her without warning.

Unrayed she stood, with long hair streaming,
A cockle-shell cupped in her warm hands,
Her axe propped idly on a stone.

No awe possessed me, only a great grief;
Wanly she smiled, but would not lift her eyes
(As a young girl will greet the stranger).
I stood upright, a head taller than she.
'See who has come,' said I.

She answered: 'If I lift my eyes to yours
And our eyes marry, man, what then?
Will they engender my son Darien?
Swifter than wind, with straight and nut-brown hair,
Tall, slender-shanked, grey-eyed, untameable;
Never was born, nor ever will be born
A child to equal my son Darien,
Guardian of the hid treasures of your world.'

I knew then by the trembling of her hands
For whom that flawless blade would sweep:
My own oracular head, swung by its hair.

'Mistress,' I cried, 'the times are evil
And you have charged me with their remedy.
O, where my head is now, let nothing be
But a clay counterfeit with nacre blink:
Only look up, so Darien may be born!

'He is the northern star, the spell of knowledge,
Pride of all hunters and all fishermen,
Your deathless fawn, an eaglet of your eyrie,
The topmost branch of your unfellable tree,
A tear streaking the summer night,
The new green of my hope.'
                                            Lifting her eyes,
She held mine for a lost eternity.
'Sweetheart,' said I, 'strike now, for Darien's sake!'

THE PORTRAIT

She speaks always in her own voice
Even to strangers; but those other women
Exercise their borrowed, or false, voices
Even on sons and daughters.

She can walk invisibly at noon
Along the high road; but those other women
Gleam phosphorescent – broad hips and gross fingers –
Down every lampless alley.

She is wild and innocent, pledged to love
Through all disaster; but those other women
Decry her for a witch or a common drab
And glare back when she greets them.

Here is her portrait, gazing sidelong at me,
The hair in disarray, the young eyes pleading:
'And you, love? As unlike those other men
As I those other women?'

PROMETHEUS

Close bound in a familiar bed
All night I tossed, rolling my head;
Now dawn returns in vain, for still
The vulture squats on her warm hill.

I am in love as giants are
That dote upon the evening star,
And this lank bird is come to prove
The intractability of love.

Yet still, with greedy eye half shut,
Rend the raw liver from its gut:
Feed, jealousy, do not fly away —
If she who fetched you also stay.

THE STRAW

Peace, the wild valley streaked with torrents,
A hoopoe perched on his warm rock. Then why
This tremor of the straw between my fingers?

What should I fear? Have I not testimony
In her own hand, signed with her own name
That my love fell as lightning on her heart?

These questions, bird, are not rhetorical.
Watch how the straw twitches and leaps
As though the earth quaked at a distance.

Requited love; but better unrequited
If this chance instrument gives warning
Of cataclysmic anguish far away.

Were she at ease, warmed by the thought of me,
Would not my hand stay steady as this rock?
Have I undone her by my vehemence?

DIALOGUE ON THE HEADLAND

SHE: You'll not forget these rocks and what I told you?

HE: How could I? Never: whatever happens.

SHE: What do you think might happen?
Might you fall out of love? – did you mean that?

HE: Never, never! 'Whatever' was a sop
For jealous listeners in the shadows.

SHE: You haven't answered me. I asked:
'What do you think might happen?'

HE: Whatever happens: though the skies should fall
Raining their larks and vultures in our laps –

SHE: 'Though the seas turn to slime' – say that –
'Though water-snakes be hatched with six heads.'

HE: Though the seas turn to slime, or tower
In an arching wave above us, three miles high –

SHE: 'Though she should break with you' – dare you say
that? –
'Though she deny her words on oath.'

HE: I had that in my mind to say, or nearly,
It hurt so much I choked it back.

SHE: How many other days can't you forget?
How many other loves and landscapes?

HE: You are jealous?

SHE: Damnably.

HE: The past is past.

SHE: And this?

HE: Whatever happens, this goes on.

SHE: Without a future? Sweetheart, tell me now:
What do you want of me? I must know that.

HE: Nothing that isn't freely mine already.

SHE: Say what is freely yours and you shall have it.

HE: Nothing that, loving you, I could dare take.

SHE: O, for an answer with no 'nothing' in it!

HE: Then give me everything that's left.
SHE: Left after what?
HE: After whatever happens:
     Skies have already fallen, seas are slime,
     Watersnakes poke and peer six-headedly –
SHE: And I lie snugly in the Devil's arms.
HE: I said: 'Whatever happens.' Are you crying?
SHE: You'll not forget me – ever, ever, ever?

A LOST JEWEL

Who on your breast pillows his head now,
Jubilant to have won
The heart beneath on fire for him alone,

At dawn will hear you, plagued by nightmare,
Mumble and weep
About some blue jewel you were sworn to keep.

Wake, blink, laugh out in reassurance,
Yet your tears will say:
'It was not mine to lose or give away.

'For love it shone – never for the madness
Of a strange bed –
Light on my finger, fortune in my head.'

Roused by your naked grief and beauty,
For lust he will burn:
'Turn to me, sweetheart! Why do you not turn?'

175

THE BLUE-FLY

Five summer days, five summer nights,
The ignorant, loutish, giddy blue-fly
Hung without motion on the cling peach,
Humming occasionally: 'O my love, my fair one!'
     As in the *Canticles*.

Magnified one thousand times, the insect
Looks farcically human; laugh if you will!
Bald head, stage-fairy wings, blear eyes,
A caved-in chest, hairy black mandibles,
     Long spindly thighs.

The crime was detected on the sixth day.
What then could be said or done? By anyone?
It would have been vindictive, mean and what-not
To swat that fly for being a blue-fly,
     For debauch of a peach.

Is it fair, either, to bring a microscope
To bear on the case, even in search of truth?
Nature, doubtless, has some compelling cause
To glut the carriers of her epidemics –
     Nor did the peach complain.

SPOILS

When all is over and you march for home,
The spoils of war are easily disposed of:
Standards, weapons of combat, helmets, drums
May decorate a staircase or a study,
While lesser gleanings of the battlefield –
Coins, watches, wedding-rings, gold teeth and such –
Are sold anonymously for solid cash.

The spoils of love present a different case,
When all is over and you march for home:
That lock of hair, these letters and the portrait
May not be publicly displayed; nor sold;
Nor burned; nor returned (the heart being obstinate) –
Yet never dare entrust them to a safe
For fear they burn a hole through two-foot steel.

THE FACE IN THE MIRROR

Grey haunted eyes, absent-mindedly glaring
From wide, uneven orbits; one brow drooping
Somewhat over the eye
Because of a missile fragment still inhering,
Skin deep, as a foolish record of old-world fighting.

Crookedly broken nose – low tackling caused it;
Cheeks, furrowed; coarse grey hair, flying frenetic;
Forehead, wrinkled and high;
Jowls, prominent; ears, large; jaw, pugilistic;
Teeth, few; lips, full and ruddy; mouth, ascetic.

I pause with razor poised, scowling derision
At the mirrored man whose beard needs my attention,
And once more ask him why
He still stands ready, with a boy's presumption,
To court the queen in her high silk pavilion.

GRATITUDE FOR A NIGHTMARE

His appearances are incalculable,
His strength terrible,
I do not know his name.

Huddling pensive for weeks on end, he
Gives only random hints of life, such as
Strokes of uncomfortable coincidence.

To eat heartily, dress warmly, lie snugly
And earn respect as a leading citizen
Granted long credit at all shops and inns –

How dangerous! I had feared this shag demon
Would not conform with my conformity
And in some leaner belly make his lair.

But now in dream he suddenly bestrides me . . .
'All's well,' I groan, and fumble for a light,
Brow bathed in sweat, heart pounding.

THE NAKED AND THE NUDE

For me, the naked and the nude
(By lexicographers construed
As synonyms that should express
The same deficiency of dress
Or shelter) stand as wide apart
As love from lies, or truth from art.

Lovers without reproach will gaze
On bodies naked and ablaze;
The Hippocratic eye will see
In nakedness, anatomy;
And naked shines the Goddess when
She mounts her lion among men.

The nude are bold, the nude are sly
To hold each treasonable eye.
While draping by a showman's trick
Their dishabille in rhetoric,
They grin a mock-religious grin
Of scorn at those of naked skin.

The naked, therefore, who compete
Against the nude may know defeat;
Yet when they both together tread
The briary pastures of the dead,
By Gorgons with long whips pursued,
How naked go the sometime nude!

RHEA

On her shut lids the lightning flickers,
Thunder explodes above her bed,
An inch from her lax arm the rain hisses;
Discrete she lies,

Not dead but entranced, dreamlessly
With slow breathing, her lips curved
In a half-smile archaic, her breast bare,
Hair astream.

The house rocks, a flood suddenly rising
Bears away bridges: oak and ash
Are shivered to the roots – royal green timber.
She nothing cares.

(Divine Augustus, trembling at the storm,
Wrapped sealskin on his thumb; divine Gaius
Made haste to hide himself in a deep cellar,
Distraught by fear.)

Rain, thunder, lightning: pretty children.
'Let them play,' her mother-mind repeats;
'They do no harm, unless from high spirits
Or by mishap.'

WOMAN AND TREE

To love one woman, or to sit
    Always beneath the same tall tree,
Argues a certain lack of wit
    Two steps from imbecility.

A poet, therefore, sworn to feed
    On every food the senses know,
Will claim the inexorable need
    To be Don Juan Tenorio.

Yet if, miraculously enough,
    (And why set miracles apart?)
Woman and tree prove of a stuff
    Wholly to glamour his wild heart?

And if such visions from the void
    As shone in fever there, or there,
Assemble, hold and are enjoyed
    On climbing one familiar stair . . .?

To change and chance he took a vow,
    As he thought fitting. None the less,
What of a phoenix on the bough,
    Or a sole woman's fatefulness?

BEAUTY IN TROUBLE

Beauty in trouble flees to the good angel
    On whom she can rely
To pay her cab-fare, run a steaming bath,
    Poultice her bruised eye;

Will not at first, whether for shame or caution,
    Her difficulty disclose;
Until he draws a cheque book from his plumage,
    Asking how much she owes.

(Breakfast in bed: coffee and marmalade,
    Toast, eggs, orange-juice,
After a long, sound sleep – the first since when? –
    And no word of abuse.)

Loves him less only than her saint-like mother,
    Promises to repay
His loans and most seraphic thoughtfulness
    A million-fold one day.

Beauty grows plump, renews her broken courage
    And, borrowing ink and pen,
Writes a news–letter to the evil angel
    (Her first gay act since when?):

The fiend who beats, betrays and sponges on her,
    Persuades her white is black,
Flaunts vespertilian wing and cloven hoof;
    And soon will fetch her back.

Virtue, good angel, is its own reward:
    Your guineas were well spent.
But would you to the marriage of true minds
    Admit impediment?

A PLEA TO BOYS AND GIRLS

You learned Lear's *Nonsense Rhymes* by heart, not rote;
    You learned Pope's *Iliad* by rote, not heart;
These terms should be distinguished if you quote
    My verses, children – keep them poles apart –
And call the man a liar who says I wrote
    All that I wrote in love, for love of art.

AROUND THE MOUNTAIN

Some of you may know, others perhaps can guess
  How it is to walk all night through summer rain
(Thin rain that shrouds a beneficent full moon),
  To circle a mountain, and then limp home again.

The experience varies with a traveller's age
  And bodily strength, and strength of the love affair
That harries him out of doors in steady drizzle,
  With neither jacket nor hat, and holds him there.

Still, let us concede some common elements:
  Wild-fire that, until midnight, burns his feet;
And surging rankly up, strong on the palate,
  Scents of July, imprisoned by long heat.

Add: the sub-human, black tree-silhouettes
  Against a featureless pale pall of sky;
Unseen, gurgling water; the bulk and menace
  Of entranced houses; a wraith wandering by.

Milestones, each one witness of a new mood –
  Anger, desperation, grief, regret;
Her too-familiar face that whirls and totters
  In memory, never willing to stay set.

Whoever makes the desired turning-point,
  Which means another fifteen miles to go,
Learns more from dawn than love, so far, has taught him:
  Especially the false dawn, when cocks first crow.

Those last few miles are easy: being assured
   Of the truth, why should he fabricate fresh lies?
His house looms up; the eaves drip drowsily;
   The windows blaze to a resolute sunrise.

FORBIDDEN WORDS

There are some words carry a curse with them:
Smooth-trodden, abstract, slippery vocables.
They beckon like a path of stepping stones;
But lift them up and watch what writhes or scurries!

Concepts barred from the close language of love –
Darling, you use no single word of the list,
Unless ironically in truth's defence
To volley it back against the abstractionist.

Which is among your several holds on my heart;
For you are no uninstructed child of Nature,
But passed in schools and attained the laurel wreath:
Only to trample it on Apollo's floor.

IV

LYCEIA

All the wolves of the forest
Howl for Lyceia,
Crowding together
In a close circle,
Tongues a-loll.

A silver serpent
Coiled at her waist
And a quiver at knee,
She combs fine tresses
With a fine comb:

Wolf-like, woman-like,
Gazing about her,
Greeting the wolves;
Partial to many,
Yet masked in pride.

The young wolves snarl,
They snap at one another
Under the moon.
'Beasts, be reasonable,
My beauty is my own!'

Lyceia has a light foot
For a weaving walk.
Her archer muscles
Warn them how tightly
She can stretch the string.

I question Lyceia,
Whom I find posted
Under the pine trees
One early morning:
'What do the wolves learn?'

'They learn only envy,'
Lyceia answers,
'Envy and hope.
Hope and chagrin.
Would you howl too
In that wolfish circle?'
She laughs as she speaks.

SYMPTOMS OF LOVE

Love is a universal migraine,
A bright stain on the vision
Blotting out reason.

Symptoms of true love
Are leanness, jealousy,
Laggard dawns;

Are omens and nightmares –
Listening for a knock,
Waiting for a sign:

For a touch of her fingers
In a darkened room,
For a searching look.

Take courage, lover!
Could you endure such grief
At any hand but hers?

UNDER THE OLIVES

We never would have loved had love not struck
Swifter than reason, and despite reason:
Under the olives, our hands interlocked,
We both fell silent:
Each listened for the other's answering
Sigh of unreasonableness –
Innocent, gentle, bold, enduring, proud.

APPLE ISLAND

Though cruel seas like mountains fill the bay,
Wreckiňg the quayside huts,
Salting our vineyards with tall showers of spray;

And though the moon shines dangerously clear,
Fixed in another cycle
Than the sun's progress round the felloe'd year;

And though I may not hope to dwell apart
With you on Apple Island
Unless my breast be docile to the dart –

Why should I fear your element, the sea,
Or the full moon, your mirror,
Or the halved apple from your holy tree?

TROUGHS OF SEA

'Do you delude yourself?' a neighbour asks,
Dismayed by my abstraction.
But though love cannot question love
Nor need deny its need,

Pity the man who finds a rebel heart
Under his breastbone drumming
Which reason warns him he should drown
In midnight wastes of sea.

Now as he stalks between tormented pines
(The moon in her last quarter)
A lissom spectre glides ahead
And utters not a word.

Waves tasselled with dark weed come rearing up
Like castle walls, disclosing
Deep in their troughs a ribbed sea-floor
To break his bones upon.

– Clasp both your hands under my naked foot
And press hard, as I taught you:
A trick to mitigate the pangs
Either of birth or love.

THE DEATH GRAPPLE

Lying between your sheets, I challenge
A watersnake in a swoln cataract
Or a starved lioness among drifts of snow.

Yet dare it out, for after each death grapple,
Each gorgon stare borrowed from very hate,
A childish innocent smile touches your lips,
Your eyelids droop, fearless and careless,
And sleep remoulds the lineaments of love.

PATIENCE

Almost I could prefer
A flare of anger
To your dumb signal of displeasure.

Must it be my task
To assume the mask
Of not desiring what I may not ask?

On a wide bed,
Both arms outspread,
I watch the spites do battle in my head,

Yet know this sickness
For stubborn weakness
Unconsonant with your tenderness.

O, to be patient
As you would have me patient:
Patient for a thousand nights, patient!

TURN OF THE MOON

Never forget who brings the rain
In swarthy goatskin bags from a far sea:
It is the Moon as she turns, repairing
Damages of long drought and sunstroke.

Never count upon rain, never foretell it,
For no power can bring rain
Except the Moon as she turns; and who can rule her?

She is prone to delay the necessary floods,
Lest such a gift might become obligation,
A month, or two, or three; then suddenly
Not relenting but by way of whim
Will perhaps conjure from the cloudless west
A single rain-drop to surprise with hope
Each haggard, upturned face.

Were the Moon a Sun, we would count upon her
To bring rain seasonably as she turned;
Yet no one thinks to thank the regular Sun
For shining fierce in summer, mild in winter –
Why should the Moon so drudge?

But if one night she brings us, as she turns,
Soft, steady, even, copious rain
That harms no leaf nor flower, but gently falls
Hour after hour, sinking to the tap roots,
And the sodden earth exhales at dawn
A long sigh scented with pure gratitude,
Such rain – the first rain of our lives, it seems,
Neither foretold, cajoled, nor counted on –
Is woman giving as she loves.

SELDOM YET NOW

Seldom yet now: the quality
Of this fierce love between us –
Seldom the encounter,
The presence always,
Free of oath or promise.

And if we were not so
But birds of similar plumage caged
In the peace of every day,
Would we still conjure wildfire up
From common earth, as now?

SURGICAL WARD: MEN

Something occurred after the operation
To scare the surgeons (though no fault of theirs),
Whose reassurance did not fool me long.
Beyond the shy, concerned faces of nurses
A single white-hot eye, focusing on me,
Forced sweat in rivers down from scalp to belly.
I whistled, gasped or sang, with blanching knuckles
Clutched at my bed-grip almost till it cracked:
Too proud, still, to let loose Bedlamite screeches
And bring the charge-nurse scuttling down the aisle
With morphia-needle levelled . .
Lady Morphia –

Her scorpion kiss and dark gyrating dreams –
She in mistrust of whom I dared out-dare,
Two minutes longer than seemed possible,
Pain, that unpurposed, matchless elemental
Stronger than fear or grief, stranger than love.

JOAN AND DARBY

My friends are those who find agreement with me
In large measure, but not absolutely.
Little children, parasites and God
May flatter me with absolute agreement –
For no one lives more cynical than God.

As for my love, I gifted my heart to her
Twenty years ago, without proviso,
And in return she gifted hers to me;
Yet still they beat as two, unyielding in
Their honest, first reluctance to agree.

Other seasons, other thoughts and reasons,
Other fears or phases of the moon:
In loving-kindness we grow grey together –
Like Joan and Darby in their weather-lodge
Who never venture out in the same weather.

SONG: COME, ENJOY YOUR SUNDAY!

Into your outstretched hands come pouring
Gifts by the cornucopiaful –
    What else is lacking?
Come, enjoy your Sunday
While yet you may!

Cease from unnecessary labours,
Saunter into the green world stretching far,
    Light a long cigar,
Come, enjoy your Sunday
While yet you may!

What more, what more? You fended off disaster
In a long war, never acknowledging
    Any man as master;
Come, enjoy your Sunday
While yet you may!

Are you afraid of death? But death is nothing:
The leaden seal set on a filled flask.
    If it be life you ask,
Come, enjoy your Sunday
While yet you may!

On a warm sand dune now, sprawling at ease
With little in mind, learn to despise the sea's
    Unhuman restlessness:
Come, enjoy your Sunday
While yet you may!

RUBY AND AMETHYST

Two women: one as good as bread,
   Bound to a sturdy husband.
Two women: one as rare as myrrh,
   Bound only to herself.

Two women: one as good as bread,
   Faithful to every promise.
Two women: one as rare as myrrh,
   Who never pledges faith.

The one a flawless ruby wears
   But with such innocent pleasure
A stranger's eye might think it glass
   And take no closer look.

Two women: one as good as bread,
   The noblest of the city.
Two women: one as rare as myrrh,
   Who needs no public praise.

The pale rose-amethyst on her breast
   Has such a garden in it
Your eye could trespass there for hours,
   And wonder, and be lost.

About her head a swallow wheels
   Nor ever breaks the circuit:
Glory and awe of womanhood
   Still undeclared to man.

Two women: one as good as bread,
    Resistant to all weathers.
Two women: one as rare as myrrh,
    Her weather still her own.

HORIZON

On a clear day how thin the horizon
Drawn between sea and sky,
Between sea-love and sky-love;
And after sunset how debatable
Even for an honest eye.

'Do as you will tonight,'
Said she, and so he did
By moonlight, candlelight,
Candlelight and moonlight,
While pillowed clouds the horizon hid.

Knowing-not-knowing that such deeds must end
In a curse which lovers long past weeping for
Had heaped upon him: she would be gone one
    night
With his familiar friend,
Granting him leave her beauty to explore
By moonlight, candlelight,
Candlelight and moonlight.

IN HER PRAISE

This they know well: the Goddess yet abides.
Though each new lovely woman whom she rides,
Straddling her neck a year or two or three,
Should sink beneath such weight of majesty
And, groping back to humankind, gainsay
The headlong power that whitened all her way
With a broad track of trefoil – leaving you,
Her chosen lover, ever again thrust through
With daggers, your purse rifled, your rings gone –
Nevertheless they call you to live on
To parley with the pure, oracular dead,
To hear the wild pack whimpering overhead,
To watch the moon tugging at her cold tides.
Woman is mortal woman. She abides.

A RESTLESS GHOST

Alas for obstinate doubt: the dread
Of error in supposing my heart freed,
All care for her stone dead!
Ineffably will shine the hills and radiant coast
Of early morning when she is gone indeed,
Her divine elements disbanded, disembodied
And through the misty orchards in love spread –
When she is gone indeed –
But still among them moves her restless ghost.

BETWEEN MOON AND MOON

In the last sad watches of night
Hardly a sliver of light will remain
To edge the guilty shadow of a waned moon
That dawn must soon devour.
                          Thereafter, another
Crescent queen shall arise with power –
So wise a beauty never yet seen, say I:
A true creature of moon, though not the same
In nature, name or feature –
Her innocent eye rebuking inconstancy
As if Time itself should die and disappear.

So was it ever. She is here again, I sigh.

BEWARE, MADAM!

Beware, madam, of the witty devil,
The arch intriguer who walks disguised
In a poet's cloak, his gay tongue oozing evil.

Would you be a Muse? He will so declare you,
Pledging his blind allegiance,
Yet remain secret and uncommitted.

Poets are men: are single-hearted lovers
Who adore and trust beyond all reason,
Who die honourably at the gates of hell.

The Muse alone is licensed to do murder
And to betray: weeping with honest tears
She thrones each victim in her paradise.

But from this Muse the devil borrows an art
That ill becomes a man. Beware, madam:
He plots to strip you bare of woman-pride.

He is capable of seducing your twin-sister
On the same pillow, and neither she nor you
Will suspect the act, so close a glamour he sheds.

Alas, being honourably single-hearted,
You adore and trust beyond all reason,
Being no more a Muse than he a poet.

THE BROKEN GIRTH

Bravely from Fairyland he rode, on furlough,
Astride a tall bay given him by the Queen
From whose couch he had leaped not a half-hour since,
Whose lilies-of-the-valley shone from his helm.

But alas, as he paused to assist five Ulstermen
Sweating to raise a recumbent Ogham pillar,
Breach of a saddle-girth tumbled Oisín
To common Irish earth. And at once, it is said,
Old age came on him with grief and frailty.

So Patrick asked: would he not confess the Christ? —
Which for that Lady's sake he loathed to do,
But northward loyally turned his eyes in death.
It was Fenians bore the unshriven corpse away
For burial, keening.
                              Curse me all squint-eyed monks
Who misconstrue the passing of Finn's son:
Old age, not Fairyland, was his delusion.

THREE SONGS FOR THE LUTE

I

Truth Is Poor Physic
A wild beast falling sick
Will find his own best physic —
    Herb, berry, root of tree
Or wholesome salt to lick —
    And so run free.

But this I know at least
Better than a wild beast:
    That should I fall love-sick
And the wind veer to East,
    Truth is poor physic.

II

In Her Only Way
When her need for you dies
    And she wanders apart,
Never rhetoricize
    On the faithless heart,

But with manlier virtue
    Be content to say
She both loved you and hurt you
    In her only way.

III

Hedges Freaked with Snow
No argument, no anger, no remorse,
    No dividing of blame.
There was poison in the cup – why should we ask
    From whose hand it came?

No grief for our dead love, no howling gales
    That through darkness blow,
But the smile of sorrow, a wan winter landscape,
    Hedges freaked with snow.

A TIME OF WAITING

The moment comes when my sound senses
Warn me to keep the pot at a quiet simmer,
Conclude no rash decisions, enter into
No random friendships, check the runaway tongue
And fix my mind in a close caul of doubt –
Which is more difficult, maybe, than to face
Night-long assaults of lurking furies.

The pool lies almost empty; I watch it nursed
By a thin stream. Such idle intervals
Are from waning moon to the new – a moon always
Holds the cords of my heart. Then patience, hands;
Dabble your nerveless fingers in the shallows;
A time shall come when she has need of them.

EXPECT NOTHING

Give, ask for nothing, hope for nothing,
Subsist on crumbs, though scattered casually
Not for you (she smiles) but for the birds.
Though only a thief's diet, it staves off
Dire starvation, nor does she grow fat
On the bread she crumbles, while the lonely truth
Of love is honoured, and her word pledged.

AT BEST, POETS

Woman with her forests, moons, flowers, waters,
And watchful fingers:
We claim no magic comparable to hers –
At best, poets; at worst, sorcerers.

SHE IS NO LIAR

She is no liar, yet she will wash away
Honey from her lips, blood from her shadowy hand,
And, dressed at dawn in clean white robes will say,
Trusting the ignorant world to understand:
'Such things no longer are; this is today.'

A LAST POEM

A last poem, and a very last, and yet another –
O, when can I give over?
Must I drive the pen until blood bursts from my nails
And my breath fails and I shake with fever,
Or sit well wrapped in a many-coloured cloak
Where the moon shines new through Castle Crystal?
Shall I never hear her whisper softly:
'But this is truth written by you only,
And for me only; therefore, love, have done'?

JUDGEMENT OF PARIS

What if Prince Paris, after taking thought,
Had not adjudged the apple to Aphrodite
But, instead, had favoured buxom Hera,
Divine defendress of the marriage couch?
What if Queen Helen had been left to squander
Her beauty upon the thralls of Menelaus,
Hector to die unhonoured in his bed,
Penthesileia to hunt a poorer quarry,
The bards to celebrate a meaner siege?
Could we still have found the courage, you and I,
To embark together for Cranaë
And consummate our no less fateful love?

MAN DOES, WOMAN IS

Studiously by lamp-light I appraised
The palm of your hand, its heart-line
Identical with its head-line;
And you appraised the approving frown.

I spread my cards face-upwards on the table,
Not challenging you for yours.
Man does; but woman is –
Can a gamester argue with his luck?

THE THREE-FACED

Who calls her two-faced? Faces, she has three:
The first inscrutable, for the outer world;
The second shrouded in self-contemplation;
The third, her face of love,
Once for an endless moment turned on me.

TO BEGUILE AND BETRAY

To beguile and betray, though pardonable in women,
Slowly quenches the divine need-fire
By true love kindled in them. Have you not watched
The immanent Goddess fade from their brows
When they make private to her mysteries
Some whip-scarred rogue from the hulks, some painted
    clown
From the pantomime – and afterwards accuse you
Of jealous hankering for the mandalot
Rather than horror and sick foreboding
That she will never return to the same house?

DANCE OF WORDS

To make them move, you should start from lightning
And not forecast the rhythm: rely on chance,
Or so-called chance for its bright emergence
Once lightning interpenetrates the dance.

Grant them their own traditional steps and postures
But see they dance it out again and again
Until only lightning is left to puzzle over –
The choreography plain, and the theme plain.

THE OLEASTER

Each night for seven nights beyond the gulf
A storm raged, out of hearing, and crooked flashes
Of lightning animated us. Before day-break
Rain fell munificently for the earth's need . . .

No, here they never plant the sweet olive
As some do (bedding slips in a prepared trench),
But graft it on the club of Hercules
The savage, inexpugnable oleaster
Whose roots and bole bunching from limestone crannies
Sprout impudent shoots born only to be lopped
Spring after Spring. Theirs is a loveless berry . . .

By mid-day we walk out, with naked feet,
Through pools on the road, gazing at waterfalls
Or a line of surf, but mostly at the trees
Whose elegant branches rain has duly blackened
And pressed their crowns to a sparkling silver.

ENDLESS PAVEMENT

In passage along an endless, eventless pavement,
None but the man in love, as he turns to stare
At the glazed eyes flickering past, will remain aware
Of his own, assured, meticulous, rustic tread –
As if pavement were pebbles, or rocks overgrown by
      grasses;
And houses, trees with birds flying overhead.

THE BLACK GODDESS

Silence, words into foolishness fading,
Silence prolonged, of thought so secret
We hush the sheep-bells and the loud cicada.

And your black agate eyes, wide open, mirror
The released firebird beating his way
Down a whirled avenue of blues and yellows.

Should I not weep? Profuse the berries of love,
The speckled fish, the filberts and white ivy
Which you, with a half-smile, bestow
On your delectable broad land of promise
For me, who never before went gay in plumes.

GOOD NIGHT TO THE OLD GODS

Good night, old gods, all this long year so faint
You propped your heavy eyelids up with shells!
Though once we honoured you who ruled this land
One hundred generations and ten more,
Our mood has changed: you dribble at the mouth,
Your dark-blue fern-tattoos are faded green,
Your thunderous anger wanes to petulance,
And love to groanings of indifference.
What most you crave is rest in a rock-cave,
Seasonally aroused by raucous gulls
Or swallows, nodding off once more to sleep.

We lay you in a row with cool palm wine
Close at your elbows, should you suffer thirst,
And breadfruit piled on rushes by your feet;
But will not furnish you a standing guard –
We have fish to net and spear, taro to hoe,
Pigs to fatten, coco-trees to climb;
Nor are our poets so bedulled in spirit
They would mount a platform, praising in worn verse
Those fusillades of lightning hurled by you
At giants in a first day-break of time:
Whom you disarmed and stretched in a rock-cave
Not unlike this – you have forgotten where.

THE SWEET-SHOP ROUND THE CORNER

The child dreaming along a crowded street
Lost hold of his mother, who had turned to greet
Some neighbour, and mistakenly matched his tread
With a strange woman's. 'Buy me sweets,' he said,
Waving his hand, which he found warmly pressed;
So dragged her on, boisterous and self-possessed:
'The sweet-shop's round the corner!' Both went in,
And not for a long while did the child begin
To feel a dread that something had gone wrong:
Were Mother's legs so lean, or her shoes so long,
Or her skirt so patched, or her hair tousled and grey?
Why did she twitter in such a ghostly way?
'O Mother, are you dead?'
                                What else could a child say?

BETWEEN HYSSOP AND AXE

To know our destiny is to know the horror
Of separation, dawn oppressed by night:
Is, between hyssop and axe, boldly to prove
That gifted, each, with singular need for freedom
And haunted, both, by spectres of reproach,
We may yet house together without succumbing
To the low fever of domesticity
Or to the lunatic spin of aimless flight.

THE IMPOSSIBLE

Dear love, since the impossible proves
  Our sole recourse from this distress,
Claim it: the ebony ritual-mask of no
  Cannot outstare a living yes.

Claiming it without despond or hate
  Or greed; but in your gentler tone
Say: 'This is ours, the impossible,' and silence
  Will give consent it is ours alone.

The impossible has wild-cat claws
  Which you would rather meet and die
Than commit love to time's curative venom
  And break our oath; for so would I.

ARREARS OF MOONLIGHT

My heart lies wrapped in red under your pillow,
My body wanders banished among the stars;
On one terrestrial pretext or another
You still withhold the extravagant arrears
Of moonlight that you owe us,
Though the owl whoops from a far olive branch
His brief, monotonous, night-long reminder.

WHAT DID YOU SAY?

She listened to his voice urgently pleading,
So captivated by his eloquence
She saw each word in its own grace and beauty
Drift like a flower down that clear-flowing brook,
And draw a wake of multicoloured bubbles.
But when he paused, intent on her reply,
She could stammer only: 'Love, what did you say?' –
As loath as ever to hold him in her arms
Naked, under the trees, until high day.

THE GORGE

Yonder beyond all hopes of access
Begins your queendom; here is my frontier.
Between us howl phantoms of the long dead,
But the bridge that I cross, concealed from view
Even in sunlight, and the gorge bottomless,
Swings and echoes under my strong tread
Because I have need of you.

LOVING TRUE, FLYING BLIND

How often have I said before
That no soft 'if', no 'either-or',
Can keep my obdurate male mind
From loving true and flying blind? –

Which, though deranged beyond all cure
Of temporal reason, knows for sure
That timeless magic first began
When woman bared her soul to man.

Be bird, be blossom, comet, star,
Be paradisal gates ajar,
But still, as woman, bear you must
With who alone endures your trust.

LIKE OWLS

The blind are their own brothers; we
Form an obscure fraternity
Who, though not destitute of sight
Know ourselves doomed from birth to see,
Like owls, most clearly in half light.

THE UTTER RIM

But if that Cerberus, my mind, should be
Flung to earth by the very opiate
That frees my senses for undared adventure,
Waving them wide-eyed past me to explore
Limitless hells of disintegrity,
Endless, undifferentiatable fate
Scrolled out beyond the utter rim of nowhere,
Scrolled out . . . . . .
                              who on return fail to surrender
Their memory trophies, random wisps of horror
Trailed from my shins or tangled in my hair?

IN PERSPECTIVE

What, keep love in *perspective?* – that old lie
Forced on the Imagination by the Eye
Which, mechanistically controlled, will tell
How rarely table-sides run parallel;
How distance shortens us; how wheels are found
Oval in shape far oftener than round;
How every ceiling-corner's out of joint;
How the broad highway tapers to a point –
Can all this fool us lovers? Not for long:
Even the blind will sense that something's wrong.

BOWER-BIRD

The Bower-bird improvised a cool retreat
For the hen he honoured, doing his poor best
With parrot-plumage, orchids, bones and corals,
To engage her fancy.
                              But this was no nest . . .
So, though the Penguin dropped at his hen's feet
An oval stone to signal: 'be my bride',
And though the Jackdaw's nest was glorified
With diamond rings and brooches massed inside,
It was the Bower-bird who contented me
By not equating love with matrimony.

THE WORD

The word is unspoken
Between honest lovers:
They substitute a silence
Or wave at a wild flower,
Sighing inaudibly.

That it exists indeed
Will scarcely be disputed:
The wildest of conceptions
Can be reduced to speech –
Or so the Schoolmen teach.

You and I, thronged by angels,
Learned it in the same dream
Which startled us by moonlight,
And that we still revere it
Keeps our souls aflame.

'God' is a standing question
That still negates an answer.
The Word is not a question
But simple affirmation,
The antonym of 'God'.

Who would believe this Word
Could have so long been hidden
Behind a candid smile,
A sweet but hasty kiss
And always dancing feet?

OUR SELF

When first we came together
It was no chance foreshadowing
Of a chance happy ending.
The case grows always clearer
By its own worse disorder:
However reasonably we oppose
That unquiet integer, our self, we lose.

HER BRIEF WITHDRAWAL

'Forgive me, love, if I withdraw awhile:
It is only that you ask such bitter questions,
Always another beyond the extreme last.
And the answers astound: you have entangled me
In my own mystery. Grant me a respite:
I was happier far, not asking, nor much caring,
Choosing by appetite only: self-deposed,
Self-reinstated, no one observing.
When I belittled this vibrancy of touch
And the active vengeance of these folded arms
No one could certify my powers for me
Or my saining virtue, or know that I compressed
Knots of destiny in a careless fist,
I who had passed for a foundling from the hills
Of innocent and flower-like phantasies,
Though minting silver by my mere tread . . .
Did I not dote on you, I well might strike you
For implicating me in your true dream.'

V

SONG: THOUGH ONCE TRUE LOVERS

Though once true lovers,
    We are less than friends.
What woman ever
    So ill-used her man?
That I played false
    Not even she pretends:
May God forgive her,
    For, alas, I can.

SONG: DEW-DROP AND DIAMOND

The difference between you and her
(Whom I to you did once prefer)
Is clear enough to settle:
She like a diamond shone, but you
Shine like an early drop of dew
Poised on a red rose-petal.

The dew-drop carries in its eye
Mountain and forest, sea and sky,
With every change of weather;
Contrariwise, a diamond splits
The prospect into idle bits
That none can piece together.

THE HOME-COMING

At the tangled heart of a wood I fell asleep,
Bewildered by her silence and her absence –
As though such potent lulls in love were not
Ordained by the demands of pure music.

A bird sang: 'Close your eyes, it is not for long –
Dream of what gold and crimson she will wear
In honour of your oak-brown.'

It was her hoopoe. Yet, when the spread heavens
Of my feast night glistened with shooting stars
And she walked unheralded up through the dim light
Of the home lane, I did not recognize her –
So lost a man can be
Who feeds on hopes and fears and memory.

WIGS AND BEARDS

In the bad old days a bewigged country Squire
Would never pay his debts, unless at cards,
Shot, angled, urged his pack through standing grain,
Horsewhipped his tenantry, snorted at the arts,
Toped himself under the table every night,
Blasphemed God with a cropful of God-damns,
Aired whorehouse French or lame Italian,
Set fashions of pluperfect slovenliness
And claimed seigneurial rights over all women
Who slept, imprudently, under the same roof.

Taxes and wars long ago ploughed them under –
'And serve the bastards right' the Beards agree,
Hurling their empties through the café window
And belching loud as they proceed downstairs.
Latter-day bastards of that famous stock,
They never rode a nag, nor gaffed a trout,
Nor winged a pheasant, nor went soldiering,
But remain true to the same hell-fire code
In all available particulars
And scorn to pay their debts even at cards.
Moreunder (which is to subtract, not add),
Their ancestors called themselves gentlemen
As they, in the same sense, call themselves artists.

ALL EXCEPT HANNIBAL

Trapped in a dismal marsh, he told his troops:
'No lying down, lads! Form your own mess-groups
And sit in circles, each man on the knees
Of the man behind; then nobody will freeze.'

They obeyed his orders, as the cold sun set,
Drowsing all night in one another's debt,
All except Hannibal himself, who chose
His private tree-stump – he was one of those!

TOUSLED PILLOW

She appeared in Triad – Youth, Truth, Beauty –
Full face and profiles whispering together
All night at my bed-foot.
                                And when dawn came
At last, from a tousled pillow resolutely
I made my full surrender:
'So be it, Goddess, claim me without shame
And tent me in your hair.'
                                Since when she holds me
As close as candlewick to candleflame
And from all hazards free,
My soul drawn back to its virginity.

WITHIN REASON

You have wandered widely through your own mind
And your own perfect body;
Thus learning, within reason, gentle one,
Everything that can prove worth the knowing.

A concise wisdom never attained by those
Bodiless nobodies
Who travel pen in hand through others' minds,
But without reason,
Feeding on manifold contradiction.

To stand perplexed by love's inconsequences
Like fire-flies in your hair
Or distant flashes of a summer storm:
Such are the stabs of joy you deal me
Who also wander widely through my mind
And still imperfect body.

THE YET UNSAYABLE

It was always fiercer, brighter, gentler than could be told
Even in words quickened by Truth's dark eye:
Its absence, whirlpool; its presence, deluge;
Its time, astonishment; its magnitude,
A murderous dagger-point.
                              So we surrender
Our voices to the dried and scurrying leaves
And choose our own long-predetermined path
From the unsaid to the yet unsayable
In silence of love and love's temerity.

THE NARROW SEA

With you for mast and sail and flag,
And anchor never known to drag,
Death's narrow but oppressive sea
Looks not unnavigable to me.

THE OLIVE-YARD

Now by a sudden shift of eye
The hitherto exemplary world
Takes on immediate wildness
And birds, trees, winds, the very letters
Of our childhood's alphabet, alter
Into rainbowed mysteries.

Flesh is no longer flesh, but power;
Numbers, no longer arithmetical,
Dance like lambs, fly like doves;
And silence falls at last, though silken branches
Gently heave in the near olive-yard
And vague cloud labours on.

Whose was the stroke of summer genius
Flung from a mountain fastness
Where the griffon-vulture soars
That let us read our shrouded future
As easily as a book of prayer
Spread open on the knee?

SONG: BEYOND GIVING

There is a giving beyond giving:
    Yours to me
Who awoke last night, hours before the dawn,
    Set free
By one intolerable lightning stroke
    That ripped the sky
To understand what love withholds in love
    And why.

COMPACT

My love for you, though true, wears the extravagance of
    centuries;
Your love for me is fragrant, simple and millennial.
Smiling without a word, you watch my extravagances
    pass;
To check them would be presumptuous and unmaidenly –
As it were using me like an ill-bred schoolboy.

Dear Live-apart, when I sit confused by the active spites
Tormenting me with too close sympathy for fools,
Too dark a rage against hidden plotters of evil,
Too sour a mind, or soused with sodden wool-bales –
I turn my eyes to the light smoke drifting from your fire.

Our settled plan has been: never to make plans –
The future, present and past being already settled
Beyond review or interpretative conjecture
By the first decision of truth that we clasped hands upon:
To conserve a purity of soul each for the other.

IN THE NAME OF VIRTUE

In the name of Virtue, girl,
Why must you try so hard
In the hard name of Virtue?
Is not such trying, questioning?
Such questioning, doubting?
Such doubting, guessing?
Such guessing, not-knowing?
Such not-knowing, not-being?
Such not-being, death?
Can death be Virtue?

Virtue is from listening
To a private angel,
An angel overheard
When the little-finger twitches –
The bold little finger
That refused education:
When the rest went to college
And philosophized on Virtue,
It neither went, nor tried.

Knowing becomes doing
When all we need to know
Is how to check our pendulum
And move the hands around
For a needed golden instant
Of the future or past –
Then start time up again
With a bold little-finger
In Virtue's easy name.

THE THEME OF DEATH

Since love is an astonished always
Challenging the long lies of history,
Yesterday when I chose the theme of death
You shook a passionate finger at me:
'Wake from your nightmare! Would you murder love?
Wake from your nightmare!'

No, sweetheart! Death is nightmare when conceived
As God's Last Judgement, or the curse of Time –
Its intransgressible bounds of destiny;
But love is an astonished always
With death as affidavit for its birth
And timeless progress.

What if these tombs and catafalques conspire,
Menacing us with gross ancestral fears,
To dissipate my living truth, and yours,
To induct us into ritual weeping?
Our love remains a still astonished always,
Pure death its witness.

THROUGH A DARK WOOD

Together, trustfully, through a dark wood –
But headed where, unless to the ancient, cruel,
Inescapable, marital pitfall
With its thorny couch for the procreation
Of love's usurpers or interlopers?
Or worse by far, should each be trapped singly
But for true-love's sake gulp down a jealousy
And grief at not having suffered jointly . . .

Together, through a dark wood, trustfully.

FIRST LOVE

Darling, if ever on some night of fever
But with your own full knowledge . . .
Darling, confess how it will be if ever
You violate your true-love pledge
Once offered me unprompted,
Which I reciprocated
Freely, fully and without restraint
Nor ever have abjured since first we kissed?
Will that prove you a liar and me a saint,
Or me a fool and you a realist?

POEM: A REMINDER

Capital letters prompting every line,
Lines printed down the centre of each page,
Clear spaces between groups of these, combine
In a convention of respectable age
To mean: 'Read carefully. Each word we chose
Has rhythm and sound and sense. This is not prose.'

                    poem: a reminder
capitallet
        –ers prompting ev
                        –ery line lines printed down the
                        cen
                        –tre of each page clear

                        spaces between

                        groups of these combine in a con
v
    e
        n
            t
                i
                    o
                    n
                        of respectable age to mean read
care
                        –fully each word we chose has

                                        rhythm and
                                        sound and
                                        sense this is
notprose

THE REITERATION

The death of love comes from reiteration:
A single line sung over and over again –
No prelude and no end.

The word is not, perhaps, 'reiteration' –
Nature herself repunctuates her seasons
With the same stars, flowers, fruits –
Though love's foolish reluctance to survive
Springs always from the same mechanical fault:
The needle jumps its groove.

TOLLING BELL

'But why so solemn when the bell tolled?'
'Did you expect me to stand up and caper?'
'Confess, what are you trying to hide from me?
Horror of death?'
                    'That seventeenth century
Skeletal effigy in the Church crypt?'
'Or is it fear, perhaps, of a second childhood?
Of incurable sickness? Or of a strange someone
Seated in your own chair at your own table?
Or worse, of that chair gone?'
                                'Why saddle me
With your own nightmares?'
                            'Fear of the other world?'

'Be your own age! What world exists but ours?'
'Distaste for funerals?'
                              'Isn't it easier
To play the unweeping corpse than the pall-bearer?'
'Why so mysterious?'
                              'Why so persistent?'
*'I only asked why you had looked solemn
When the bell tolled.'*
                              'Angered, not solemn, angered
By all parochially enforced grief.
Death is a private, ungainsayable act.'
'Privately, then, what does Death mean to you?'
'Only love's gentle sigh of consummation,
Which I have little fear of drawing too soon.'

ARROW ON THE VANE

Suddenly, at last, the bitter wind veers round
From North-East to South-West. It is at your orders;
And the arrow on our vane swings and stays true
To your direction. Nothing parts us now.
What can I say? Nothing I have not said,
However the wind blew. I more than love,
As when you drew me bodily from the dead.

THE GREEN-SAILED VESSEL

We are like doves, well-paired,
Veering across a meadow –
Children's voices below,
Their song and echo;

Like raven, wren or crow
That cry and prophesy,
What do we not foreknow,
Whether deep or shallow?

Like the tiller and prow
Of a green-sailed vessel
Voyaging, none knows how,
Between moon and shadow;

Like the restless, endless
Blossoming of a bough,
Like tansy, violet, mallow,
Like the sun's afterglow.

Of sharp resemblances
What further must I show
Until your black eyes narrow,
Furrowing your clear brow.

CLIFF AND WAVE

Since first you drew my irresistible wave
To break in foam on your immovable cliff,
We occupy the same station of being –
Not as in wedlock harboured close together,
But beyond reason, co–identical.
Now when our bodies hazard an encounter,
They dread to engage the fury of their senses,
And only in the brief dismay of parting
Will your cliff shiver or my wave falter.

THE TITLE OF POET

Poets are guardians
Of a shadowy island
With granges and forests
Warmed by the Moon.

Come back, child, come back!
You have been far away,
Housed among phantoms,
Reserving silence.

Whoever loves a poet
Continues whole hearted,
Her other loves or loyalties
Distinct and clear.

She is young, he is old
And endures for her sake
Such fears of unease
As distance provokes.

Yet how can he warn her
What natural disasters
Will plague one who dares
To neglect her poet? . . .
For the title of poet
Comes only with death.

PITY

Sickness may seem a falling out of love,
With pleas for pity – love's lean deputy.
If so, refuse me pity, wait, love on:
Never outlaw me while I yet live.
The day may come when you too, falling sick,
Implore my pity. Let me, too, refuse it
Offering you, instead, my pitiless love.

BEATRICE AND DANTE

He, a grave poet, fell in love with her.
She, a mere child, fell deep in love with love
And, being a child, illumined his whole heart.

From her clear conspect rose a whispering
With no hard words in innocency held back –
Until the day that she became a woman,

Frowning to find her love imposed upon:
A new world beaten out in her own image –
For his own deathless glory.

THE TRADITIONALIST

Respect his obstinacy of undefeat,
His hoarding of tradition,
Those hands hung loosely at his side
Always prepared for hardening into fists
Should any fool waylay him,
His feet prepared for the conquest of crags
Or a week's march to the sea.

If miracles are recorded in his presence
As in your own, remember
These are no more than time's obliquities
Gifted to men who still fall deep in love
With real women like you.

A DREAM OF FRANCES SPEEDWELL

I fell in love at my first evening party.
You were tall and fair, just seventeen perhaps,
Talking to my two sisters. I kept silent
And never since have loved a tall fair girl,
Until last night in the small windy hours
When, floating up an unfamiliar staircase
And into someone's bedroom, there I found her
Posted beside the window in half-light
Wearing that same white dress with lacy sleeves.
She beckoned. I came closer. We embraced
Inseparably until the dream faded.
Her eyes shone clear and blue . . .

Who was it, though, impersonated you?

NIGHTMARE OF SENILITY

Then must I punish you with trustfulness
Since you can trust yourself no more and dread
Fresh promptings to deceive me? Or instead
Must I reward you by deceiving you,
By heaping coals of fire on my own head?
Are truth and friendship dead?

And why must I, turning in nightmare on you,
Bawl out my lies as though to make them true?
O if this Now were once, when pitifully
You dressed my wounds, kissed and made much of me,
Though warned how things must be!

*   *   *

Very well, then: my head across the block,
A smile on your pursed lips, and the axe poised
For a merciful descent. Ministering to you
Even in my torment, praising your firm wrists,
Your resolute stance . . . How else can I protect you
From the curse my death must carry, except only
By begging you not to prolong my pain
Beyond these trivial years?
                              I am young again.
I watch you shrinking to a wrinkled hag.
Your kisses grow repulsive, your feet shuffle
And drag. Now I forget your name and forget mine . . .
No matter, they were always equally 'darling'.
Nor were my poems lies; you made them so
To mystify our friends and our friends' friends.
We were the loveliest pair: all-powerful too,
Until you came to loathe me for the hush
That our archaic legend forced on you.

MY GHOST

I held a poor opinion of myself
When young, but never bettered my opinion
(Even by comparison)
Of all my fellow-fools at school or college.

Passage of years induced a tolerance,
Even a near-affection, for myself –
Which, when you fell in love with me, amounted
(Though with my tongue kept resolutely tied)
To little short of pride.

Pride brought its punishment: thus to be haunted
By my own ghost whom, much to my disquiet,
All would-be friends and open enemies
Boldly identified and certified
As me, including him in anecdotal
Autobiographies.

Love, should you meet him in the newspapers
In planes, on trains, or at large get-togethers,
I charge you, disregard his foolish capers;
Silence him with a cold unwinking stare
Where he sits opposite you at table
And let all present watch amazed, remarking
On how little you care.

PROBLEMS OF GENDER

Circling the Sun, at a respectful distance,
Earth remains warmed, not roasted; but the Moon
Circling the Earth, at a disdainful distance,
Will drive men lunatic (should they defy her)
With seeds of wintry love, not sown for spite.

Mankind, so far, continues undecided
On the Sun's gender – grammars disagree –
As on the Moon's. Should Moon be god, or goddess:
Drawing the tide, shepherding flocks of stars
That never show themselves by broad daylight?

Thus curious problems of propriety
Challenge all ardent lovers of each sex:
Which circles which at a respectful distance,
Or which, instead, at a disdainful distance?
And who controls the regal powers of night?

LOVE AS LOVELESSNESS

What she refused him – in the name of love
And the hidden tears he shed –
She granted only to such soulless blades
As might accept her casual invitation
To a loveless bed.

Each year of the long seven gnawed at her heart,
Yet never would she lay
Tokens of his pure love under her pillow
Nor let him meet, by chance, her new bedfellow;
Thus suffering more than he.

Seven years had ended, the fierce truth was known.
Which of these two had suffered most?
Neither enquired and neither cared to boast:
'Not you, but I. It was myself alone.'
In loneliness true love burns to excess.

TIMELESS MEETING

To have attained an endless, timeless meeting
By faith in the stroke which first engaged us,
Driving two hearts improbably together
Against all faults of history
And bodily disposition –

What does this mean? Prescience of new birth?
But one suffices, having paired us off
For the powers of creation –
Lest more remain unsaid.

Nor need we make demands or deal awards
Even for a thousand years:
Who we still are we know.

Exchange of love-looks came to us unsought
And inexpressible:

To which we stand resigned.

CRUCIBLES OF LOVE

From where do poems come?
From workshops of the mind,
As do destructive armaments,
Philosophic calculations,
Schemes for man's betterment?

Or are poems born simply
From crucibles of love?
May not you and I together
Engrossed with each other
Assess their longevity?

For who else can judge merits
Or define demerits –
This remains a task for lovers
Held fast in love together
And for no others.

AT THE GATE

Where are poems? Why do I now write none?
This can mean no lack of pens, nor lack of love,
But need perhaps of an increased magic –
Where have my ancient powers suddenly gone?

Tonight I caught a glimpse of her at the gate
Grappling a monster never found before,
And jerking back its head. Had I come too late?
Her eyes blazed fire and I could look no more.

What could she hold against me? Never yet
Had I lied to her or thwarted her desire,
Rejecting prayers that I could never forget,
Stealing green leaves to light an alien fire.

WOMAN POET AND MAN POET

Woman poet and man poet
Fell in love each with the other.
It was unsafe for either
To count on sunny weather,
The body being no poet.

Yet it had been the woman
Who drew herself apart,
Cushioned on her divan,
And lent some bolder man
Her body, not her heart.

When seven long years were over
How would their story end?
No change of heart for either,
Mere changes in the weather,
A lover being no friend.

THREE TIMES IN LOVE

You have now fallen three times in love
With the same woman, first indeed blindly
And at her blind insistence;

Next with your heart alive to the danger
Of what hers might conceal, although such passion
Strikes nobly and for ever;

Now at last, deep in dream, transported
To her rose garden on the high ridge,
Assured that there she can deny you
No deserved privilege,
However controvertible or new.

THE GREEN WOODS OF UNREST

Let the weeks end as well they must
Not with clouds of scattered dust
But in pure certainty of sun –
And with gentle winds outrun
By the love that we contest
In these green woods of unrest.
You, love, are beauty's self indeed,
Never the harsh pride of need.

INDEX OF TITLES

253

INDEX OF FIRST LINES

Discover more about our forthcoming books through Penguin's FREE newspaper...

Penguin Quarterly

It's packed with:

- exciting features
- author interviews
- previews & reviews
- books from your favourite films & TV series
- exclusive competitions & much, much more...

READ MORE IN PENGUIN

In every corner of the world, on every subject under the sun, Penguin represents quality and variety – the very best in publishing today.

For complete information about books available from Penguin – including Puffins, Penguin Classics and Arkana – and how to order them, write to us at the appropriate address below. Please note that for copyright reasons the selection of books varies from country to country.

In the United Kingdom: Please write to *Dept. JC, Penguin Books Ltd, FREEPOST, West Drayton, Middlesex UB7 0BR.*

If you have any difficulty in obtaining a title, please send your order with the correct money, plus ten per cent for postage and packaging, to *PO Box No. 11, West Drayton, Middlesex UB7 0BR*

In the United States: Please write to *Consumer Sales, Penguin USA, P.O. Box 999, Dept. 17109, Bergenfield, New Jersey 07621-0120.* VISA and MasterCard holders call 1-800-253-6476 to order all Penguin titles

In Canada: Please write to *Penguin Books Canada Ltd, 10 Alcorn Avenue, Suite 300, Toronto, Ontario M4V 3B2*

In Australia: Please write to *Penguin Books Australia Ltd, P.O. Box 257, Ringwood, Victoria 3134*

In New Zealand: Please write to *Penguin Books (NZ) Ltd, Private Bag 102902, North Shore Mail Centre, Auckland 10*

In India: Please write to *Penguin Books India Pvt Ltd, 706 Eros Apartments, 56 Nehru Place, New Delhi 110 019*

In the Netherlands: Please write to *Penguin Books Netherlands bv, Postbus 3507, NL-1001 AH Amsterdam*

In Germany: Please write to *Penguin Books Deutschland GmbH, Metzlerstrasse 26, 60594 Frankfurt am Main*

In Spain: Please write to *Penguin Books S. A., Bravo Murillo 19, 1° B, 28015 Madrid*

In Italy: Please write to *Penguin Italia s.r.l., Via Felice Casati 20, I-20124 Milano*

In France: Please write to *Penguin France S. A., 17 rue Lejeune, F-31000 Toulouse*

In Japan: Please write to *Penguin Books Japan, Ishikiribashi Building, 2-5-4, Suido, Bunkyo-ku, Tokyo 112*

In Greece: Please write to *Penguin Hellas Ltd, Dimocritou 3, GR-106 71 Athens*

In South Africa: Please write to *Longman Penguin Southern Africa (Pty) Ltd, Private Bag X08, Bertsham 2013*

PENGUIN AUDIOBOOKS

⟨penguin logo⟩

A Quality of Writing that Speaks for Itself

Penguin Books has always led the field in quality publishing. Now you can listen at leisure to your favourite books, read to you by familiar voices from radio, stage and screen. Penguin Audiobooks are ideal as gifts, for when you are travelling or simply to enjoy at home. They are produced to an excellent standard, and abridgements are always faithful to the original texts. From thrillers to classic literature, biography to humour, with a wealth of titles in between, Penguin Audiobooks offer you quality, entertainment and the chance to rediscover the pleasure of listening.

You can order Penguin Audiobooks through Penguin Direct by telephoning (0181) 899 4036. The lines are open 24 hours every day. Ask for Penguin Direct, quoting your credit card details.

Published or forthcoming:

Persuasion by Jane Austen, read by Fiona Shaw

Pride and Prejudice by Jane Austen, read by Joanna David

Jericho by Dirk Bogarde, read by the author

A Period of Adjustment by Dirk Bogarde, read by the author

A Postillion Struck by Lightning by Dirk Bogarde, read by the author

A Short Walk from Harrods by Dirk Bogarde, read by the author

The Blue Afternoon by William Boyd, read by Kate Harper

Brazzaville Beach by William Boyd, read by Fiona Shaw

A Good Man in Africa by William Boyd, read by Timothy Spall

The Road to Welville by T. Coraghessan Boyle, read by the author

Jane Eyre by Charlotte Brontë, read by Juliet Stevenson

Wuthering Heights by Emily Brontë, read by Juliet Stevenson

Great Expectations by Charles Dickens, read by Hugh Laurie

Middlemarch by George Eliot, read by Harriet Walter

Zlata's Diary by Zlata Filipovič, read by Dorota Puzio

Decider by Dick Francis, read by Robert Powell

Wild Horses by Dick Francis, read by Michael Maloney

I Dreamed of Africa by Kuki Gallmann, read by Isabella Rossellini

The Prophet by Kahlil Gibran, read by Renu Setna

PENGUIN AUDIOBOOKS

Virtual Light by William Gibson, read by Peter Weller

Having It All by Maeve Haran, read by Belinda Lang

Scenes from the Sex War by Maeve Haran, read by Belinda Lang

Thunderpoint by Jack Higgins, read by Roger Moore

The Iliad by Homer, read by Derek Jacobi

More Please by Barry Humphries, read by the author

Four Past Midnight: The Sun Dog by Stephen King, read by Tim Sample

Nightmares and Dreamscapes by Stephen King, read by Whoopi Goldberg, Rob Lowe, Stephen King et al

Two Past Midnight: Secret Window, Secret Garden by Stephen King, read by James Woods

Shadow over Babylon by David Mason, read by Bob Peck

Hotel Pastis by Peter Mayle, read by Tim Pigott-Smith

Waiting to Exhale by Terry McMillan, read by the author

Murderers and Other Friends by John Mortimer, read by the author

Under the Hammer by John Mortimer, read by Tim Pigott-Smith

Bitter Medicine by Sara Paretsky, read by Christine Lahti

Guardian Angel by Sara Paretsky, read by Jane Kaczmarek

History: The Home Movie by Craig Raine, read by the author

First Offence by Nancy Taylor Rosenberg, read by Lindsay Crouse

Frankenstein by Mary Shelley, read by Richard Pasco

I Shudder at Your Touch by Michele Slung, read by Stephen King et al

The Devil's Juggler by Murray Smith, read by Kenneth Cranham

Kidnapped by Robert Louis Stevenson, read by Robbie Coltrane

The Secret History by Donna Tartt, read by Robert Sean Leonard

Bad Girls, Good Women by Rosie Thomas, read by Jenny Agutter

Asta's Book by Barbara Vine, read by Jane Lapotaire

A Dark-Adapted Eye by Barbara Vine, read by Sophie Ward

No Night is Too Long by Barbara Vine, read by Alan Cumming

READ MORE IN PENGUIN

A SELECTION OF POETRY

James Fenton Out of Danger

A collection wonderfully open to experience – of foreign places, differences, feelings and languages.

U. A. Fanthorpe Selected Poems

She is an erudite poet, rich in experience and haunted by the classical past ... fully at home in the world of the turbulent NHS, the decaying academies, and all the draughty corners of the abandoned Welfare State' – *Observer*

Yehuda Amichai Selected Poems
Translated by Chana Bloch and Stephen Mitchell

'A truly major poet ... there's a depth, breadth and weighty momentum in these subtle and delicate poems of his' – Ted Hughes

Czesław Miłosz Collected Poems 1931–1987
Winner of the 1980 Nobel Prize for Literature

'One of the greatest poets of our time, perhaps the greatest' – Joseph Brodsky

Joseph Brodsky To Urania
Winner of the 1987 Nobel Prize for Literature

Exiled from the Soviet Union in 1972, Joseph Brodsky has been universally acclaimed as the most talented Russian poet of his generation.

Paul Celan Selected Poems
Winner of the first European Translation Prize, 1990

'The English reader can now enter the hermetic universe of a German–Jewish poet who made out of the anguish of his people, things of terror and beauty' – *The Times Literary Supplement*

Geoffrey Hill Collected Poems

'Sternly formal, wry, grand, sensually direct: the contraries of a major poet' – *Observer*, Books of the Year

READ MORE IN PENGUIN

A SELECTION OF POETRY

Octavio Paz Selected Poems
Winner of the 1990 Nobel Prize for Literature

'His poetry allows us to glimpse a different and future place ... liberating and affirming' – *Guardian*

Fernando Pessoa Selected Poems

'I have sought for his shade in those Edwardian cafés in Lisbon which he haunted, for he was Lisbon's Cavafy or Verlaine' – *Sunday Times*

Roger McGough Defying Gravity

'The title poem is pure McGough – both ordinary and magical – and is perfect in its way' – *Poetry Review*

Carol Ann Duffy Selected Poems

'Carol Ann Duffy is one of the freshest and bravest talents to emerge in British poetry – any poetry – for years' – *Independent on Sunday*

John Ashbery Selected Poems

'America's leading poet ... there is a marvellous free stride in his best work, which extends the territory' – *Irish Times*

Frank O'Hara Selected Poems

With his unpremeditated, fresh style, O'Hara broke with the academic traditions of the 1950s and became the life and soul of the New York school of poets.

Dannie Abse Selected Poems

Medicine, music, the myths of Judaism, the cities of London and Cardiff – all recur in poems composed in a spare and witty style that liberates the speaking voice.

BY THE SAME AUTHOR

Wife to Mr Milton

She was sixteen and doomed to a life-long passion for a Royalist captain. He was thirty-four, a poet and Puritan, obsessed by her long golden hair. Marie Powell married John Milton in payment of a debt. It was a mismatching of bitter ineptitude, for in temperament and convictions they were worlds apart. Their marriage is the focus of this superb novel.

Count Belisarius

The Sixth Century was not a peaceful one for the Roman Empire. Invaders threatened on all frontiers. But they grew to fear and respect the name of Belisarius, horseman, archer, swordsman and military commander of incredible skill and daring. Belisarius led the Imperial armies wherever the Emperor Justinian sent him; to the Eastern Frontier on the Euphrates, across the Mediterranean to Carthage, and to Rome.

In his palace at Constantinople, Justinian plotted and intrigued, dominated by his wife, Theodora, whose spies were everywhere. Justinian hated Belisarius for his success, his nobility and his universal popularity. But Belisarius was the one man who could save the Empire . . .

Collected Short Stories

'My story is true . . . every word of it. Or when I say that my story is "true", I mean at least I am telling it in a new way . . .'

So begins 'The Shout', the tale of a man possessed by a lethal magic, perhaps Robert Graves's most famous story. This collection spans 1924–62; it takes in the worlds of love and war, history and myth, and settings as various as England, Ancient Rome and Majorca. In so far as its author asserts the truth of his stories, they can be read as episodes of autobiography, this collection forming an essential companion to *Goodbye to All That*.

BY THE SAME AUTHOR

I, Claudius

Robert Graves's magnificent reconstruction of the grandeur and
folly and vileness of early Imperial Rome is one of the most
distinguished historical novels of this generation. Its setting varies
from a Roman palace to a desert in Tripoli, a dark German forest, a
garden at Pompeii, a camp in the Balkans, the Sibyl's cavern at
Cumae, and a cliff-top on the island of Rhodes. The action is
strange, tragic and ludicrous, for Rome knows herself under a
long-standing curse – the curse of the gods with whom she broke
faith when she destroyed Carthage and lost all moral self-control.
Treachery, incest, black magic and unnatural vice flourish. Insane
cruelties are committed. And through it all moves the strange,
lovable figure of Claudius himself, despised, neglected and appar-
ently ineffective, but destined in the end to become Emperor against
his will.

Claudius the God

The hairy fifth to enslave the State,
Shall be that idiot whom all despised.

So ran the Sibylline prophecy which Claudius found among the
private papers of Augustus, and he could not fail to recognize in this
description of the last great Caesar but one, himself, the paralytic
idiot 'Clau-Clau-Claudius', as he was derisively nicknamed. In this
book he continues his historical memoirs, bringing the story from his
own acclamation as Emperor at the death of his terrible nephew,
Caligula, to his assassination in the year 54. Like its forerunner,
Claudius the God presents an astonishing picture of the grandeur and
degeneracy of first-century Rome. But Claudius himself, quite as
much as his age, comes to life in these pages – Claudius, who
survived the violent reigns of four earlier Caesars, who remained
Emperor for fourteen years, and who yet was thought by his
contemporaries to be a fool.

BY THE SAME AUTHOR

Goodbye to All That

Robert Graves's famous account of his life at Charterhouse School and as a young officer in the First World War.

'It is a permanently valuable work of literary art, and indispensable for the historian either of the First World War or of modern English poetry ... Apart, however, from its exceptional value as a war document, this book has also the interest of being one of the most candid self-portraits of a poet, warts and all, ever painted. The sketches of friends of Mr Graves, like T. E. Lawrence, are beautifully vivid' – *The Times Literary Supplement*

'From the moment of its first appearance an established classic' – John Wain in the *Observer*

The Greek Myths
(*in two volumes*)

The first modern dictionary of Greek Mythology, Robert Graves's *Greek Myths* covers in two volumes and nearly two hundred sections the Creation myths, the legends of the birth and lives of the great Olympians, the Theseus, Oedipus, and Heracles cycles, the Argonaut voyage, the tale of Troy, and much else.

All the scattered elements of each myth have been assembled into a harmonious narrative, and many variants are recorded which may help to determine their ritual or historical meanings. Full references to the classical sources, and copious indexes, make the book as valuable to the scholar as to the general reader, and a full commentary to each myth explains and interprets the classical version in the light of today's archaeological and anthropological knowledge.